Ordinary Prayer

Ordinary Prayer

Encountering God Through
Our Everyday Needs

Jeremy Michael Rios

To the Prayer Group of New Hope Alliance Church:
Without you, this book would still be a blank page in my syllabus.

TABLE OF CONTENTS

Preface

No person on earth feels adequate when it comes to his or her prayer life; we each have an ideal for prayer from which we all, woefully, fall short. Given this ingrained inadequacy, prayer is a subject about which we are all eager for help. And yet there is a real danger in offering you a book on prayer—a book that is written with the goal of helping you to pray—because the book itself might add to your sense of guilt rather than alleviate it. Perhaps we can call this danger the "cost of startup." We have a sense that really getting our prayer lives in order will take time and energy that we just can't spare. After all, our lives are busy and chaotic; it's enough, sometimes, that we are able to go to church on a Sunday at all. It is my hope, against this fearful burden, that this book will make plain and accessible what God has called each of us to do. This is why it is called *Ordinary Prayer*. It is called this because the act of prayer is not reserved for the spiritual "elite" (if such people even exist), but is the act of every ordinary believer. Toward that end, this book is meant to be a simple introduction—a primer—to prayer, and I hope that it will be useful both to the individual pray-er as well as a prayer group. In its ordinariness I hope you will come to see that prayer is a thing you can begin right now, without delay or special cost. In fact, my prayer for you is that as you read you will be led to put the book down and begin praying.

Another danger in offering a book on prayer is that you may, in the very process of reading it, become distracted, then discouraged, and then, with a sense of failure, put the book aside. The very idea of a book on prayer runs the risk of adding (even subconsciously) to the already odious debt of guilt we all feel about prayer. With this in mind, I recognize that the last thing the tired, praying people of our world need is a long book telling them how to pray; nothing, I suspect, would make our already difficult prayers less inviting or more intimidating. Against this danger, I have labored to keep this book short.

I do not mean to present myself as an "expert" on prayer. I am not convinced that experts in prayer exist. Instead, I have written this book as a Christian who has struggled to pray every bit as much as you, and it is *as* such a struggling pray-er that I have documented what God has taught me about praying over the past few years. It is entirely possible that my personal discoveries about prayer are things you have known all your lives, and that a book like this is utterly redundant. If you find that to be the case please accept these, my humblest apologies.

Jeremy M. Rios
August, 2012

I

PRAYER AND OBEDIENCE
The Prayers We Are Commanded to Pray

When I was a seminary student I began writing an instructional course on prayer. I composed a syllabus in which I planned to cover topics ranging from the Lord's Prayer, to other prewritten prayers, to mystic prayer. My hope was that, by exploring prayer in these many forms, I might fulfill Paul's command in 2 Thessalonians 5:17 to "pray continually." This particular command had always seemed like one of the more hopelessly impossible injunctions of scripture, a hyperbolic flourish similar to Jesus' commands to cut off our offending hands or pluck our offending eyes. The whole idea begged the question, Can Paul really mean that? Does he mean that we pray while sleeping? Pray while working? Pray while watching movies? Does he mean that we maintain a constant dialogue with God in our heads at all times and in all places? What is more, beyond even the logistical and spiritual difficulties of maintaining such a prayer life, there stands the opposite command of Jesus that his disciples ought, in prayer, to avoid "babbling like the heathen" (Matt. 6:7). Which is it, then? Do we pray continually, or avoid babbling? I was mired in a spiritual catch-22.

A later review of that prayer course prompted an important self-realization: while I had lots to say about mystic prayer, prayers of the Church, and the Dark Night of the Soul, I had a completely blank page when it came to petitionary prayer. What was I going to teach about that? Clearly it was part of prayer, but surely it was only an ancillary kind of prayer, not central to our faith like our need to regularly commune with and experience God in other, more exalted forms of prayer. Today, when I look back at that syllabus, its contents (or lack thereof) reveal a subtle attitude of pride that was in my heart: in many ways I felt like petitions were just too basic. What I really wanted to explore were what I considered the depths of prayer, not what seemed (to me) to be shallow and obvious. Sure, petitions were a necessary kind of prayer—like vegetables are necessary, or brushing one's teeth—but certainly they weren't the primary bread-and-butter of our faith.

I never completed much more than the syllabus for my course; other assignments and duties drew my attention from the task. In time I was called to pastor a church, and as we began to grow together in faith God began dealing with me about setting up a weekly prayer group. Of course, such a prayer group is the kind of place where people come together and *ask God to do things*. They come together and offer *petitions*— the very kind of prayer that I felt least comfortable talking about or doing. The birth of that prayer group forced me to take a long, hard look at the blank page in my syllabus. What follows in this book comes largely from my experience with them.

As we gathered and I began to seriously reflect on what we were doing God opened my eyes to a profound realization about prayer: I don't have to understand petitionary prayer, but I do have to *do* it. I don't have to comprehend the *why* of petitionary prayer, but I am commanded to pray in petitions. Jesus' teaching in the Sermon on the Mount reinforced this realization for me. There, he speaks 57 words (in Greek) that somehow encapsulate the heart of human prayer. In other words, this prayer, the Lord's Prayer, has been given to us by Jesus as the model on which we build our own prayers. Consider this prayer for a moment (Matt. 6:9b-13, author's translation):

Our Father in Heaven,
Let your Name be made holy,
Let your Kingdom come,
Let your will be done,
On earth may things be as they are in heaven.
Give to us today our bread for today,
And forgive us our sins, as we have forgiven those who sin against us,
And lead us not into temptation,
But deliver us from the Evil One.

What stands out to me now when I read these words is that each phrase of this prayer is a *request*. And while some English translations obscure this, in Greek it is clear that each clause of the prayer petitions God for something. We ask that God make His Name holy, that His Kingdom will come, for His will to be done, for things on earth to be as they are in Heaven. We ask Him for our daily sustenance, to forgive our sins, to preserve us from temptation, and to deliver us from Satan. The whole prayer, as Jesus teaches us to pray, is a series of requests; each phrase a petition.

Reflection on this passage alone was enough to cement for me the fact that praying in petitions is more a matter of obedience than understanding. This is the kind of praying I am commanded, asked, ordered by Jesus to do. I may not get it, but I *must* do it.

This change in my understanding motivated me to reevaluate what I thought about prayer in other parts of the Bible, and an investigation into the scriptural use of the word "prayer" prompted a further realization. Every time the word "pray" or a cognate is used in the Bible, it can be exchanged for the word "request" or "ask." Check it out sometime. You will find, as I did, that the biblical record of prayers is a sustained documentation of requests. Furthermore, nowhere in scripture am I commanded to "practice God's presence" or "meditate daily" (there's nothing wrong with either of these practices, by the way), but I *am* commanded to make requests daily. As these realizations accumulated they drove me to a profound re-thinking of the heart of prayer. Instead of petitions being ancillary to other kinds of prayer, I came to realize that petitions are the very heart and soul of Christian prayer. The blank page in my prayer syllabus was the most important page of all.

A final self-disclosure is in order at this point, because as the eyes of my heart were further opened I began to realize that all my efforts in prayer to date—meditation, silence, pre-written prayers, church services, the Psalms, practicing "the presence of God," praying in tongues, and praying through songs—all these were attempts to mitigate the difficulty of prayer. I had turned my attention to "alternative" prayers because I found simple, petitionary prayer to be so very difficult. By focusing my attention on prayer alternatives, I was avoiding the real issue of obedience to God's command.

This is a forgivable—or at least understandable—reaction to prayer, because prayer is a truly difficult business. And in the deepest sense prayer is difficult because our relationship with God is broken; it is difficult in the same way that talking to someone with whom you are having an argument is difficult. When you are angry with your spouse (or significant other), it becomes almost impossible to share the intimate details of your life; the argument is too fresh for intimacy. And the principle is the same in our relationship with God—we struggle to talk because we are, in some senses, in the middle of an argument.

The argument I speak of begins with Adam and Eve, whose story in Genesis 2 and 3 is a snapshot of everything that is wrong between humans and God. Before their fall, Adam and Eve are a picture of perfect relationships with each other, their work, within themselves, and with God. Adam is at peace with Eve, both of them are at peace with their work in the Garden, they feel no shame within themselves, and they enjoy perfect communion with God. But with the first couple's disobedience each of these relationships is broken. The ground is cursed for Adam—now he will struggle against it—and childrearing is similarly cursed for Eve. The man and the woman, once in communion with each other, will now fight against one another. Where they were once at peace within themselves, now they feel the burden of shame—of inner brokenness. And, of course, their relationship with God is broken as well.

Now, instead of enjoying intimacy with God, Adam and Eve hide. They hide behind bushes, and fig leaves, and they hide behind words as well. And I've always felt that something of the difficulty of prayer is more than hinted at in the first recorded conversation between Adam, Eve, and God after the Fall. There, looking ridiculous dressed in fig leaves, Adam blames Eve, and by extension God as well (who gave him Eve), for what has happened. Eve in turn blames the snake, and also by extension God (who put the snake there). And there we have it. In that first recorded conversation after the Fall, Adam and Eve were more interested in hiding than talking. And in that first conversation neither Adam nor Eve was fully honest with him or herself when talking with God. And I suspect that both of these things tragically inform our understanding of prayer's difficulty. We prefer to hide than present ourselves, and when we do present ourselves we're too busy trying to make ourselves look good—covering our problems—to be fully honest with God. Is it any wonder that we struggle to talk with Him in prayer now?

While our broken relationship with God is the central difficulty of prayer, a host of other problems swarm the believer who attempts to pray in petitions. After all, doesn't petitionary prayer raise questions about God's sovereignty? If God knows what we need before we ask Him, then why does He need us to ask at all? What's so important about our requesting things? And furthermore, why do we need to repeat ourselves, asking again and again? All of these questions, as I see them, repeat one singularly poignant question: If we believe that God is truly sovereign, isn't petitionary prayer pointless?

But the difficulties with petitions don't end there. Isn't, we might ask, petitionary prayer an act of selfishness? Isn't "asking God for things" something that is self-absorbed and pretentious? Do we really believe that the Lord of the universe needs to waste His time working to get you a new car, or a different job, or healing your sick cat, or whatever mundane and simple request you can imagine? Shouldn't we reserve His power for, you know, the "big" things? Or, on the opposite side, do we really believe that God answers prayer? Aren't grand prayers just as absurd as the small ones? And so, why would you ask God to heal the sick? Or provide for your bankrupt family? Doesn't God help those that help themselves? In either logic, the absurdity of petitionary prayer is highlighted, and the question is begged, "What's the point of praying at all?"

These are questions that I hope to answer in this book, but I raise them here to highlight the fact that prayer is difficult business. And it is difficult, primarily, because in prayer we are seeking to communicate with God despite all the brokenness of our relationship with Him. As such, prayer strikes at the heart of our spiritual inertia—the laziness, apathy and natural "drift" that draw us away from communion with God. Praying in petitions, then, is about taking those first, painful steps toward God. They are prayers that we are commanded to pray, not prayers that we are necessarily commanded to understand, and if we are not careful we will allow a host of questions—excuses, really—to obscure the issue of obedience to God's command.

Of course, this begs a further question, namely, other than out of pure obedience, why should we pray? What can the average Christian hope to gain from obeying God's commands to pray in petitions? The answer is that ordinary prayer is how we begin the process of spiritual growth, and it is in wrestling with this ordinary difficulty, with this ordinary obedience played out in the ordinary ebb and flow of our lives, that great faith is created.

This is, in principle, a thing we are all familiar with. We know that in all matters of maturity it is the small that leads to the big. The performance athlete does not walk onto the track for the first time on the day of the meet. Only a fool would show up for an exam without having opened the text or attended the lectures. We train and study in our lives— mundane, ordinary training and ordinary studying—so that we can shine at key moments.

The historic saints of the Church are athletes in faith. Examine their lives and you will quickly find that those who shone brightest were faithful in ordinary ways long before they were asked to be faithful in great ways. Those who do great things for God do a great number of small things for God that nobody ever saw. It should be no surprise, then, that this is a principle of Christian maturity that applies to us as well—that the great and shining moments of our faith are anchored in and established upon a steady, consistent, daily, plodding, and ordinary obedience. And petitionary prayer is a matter of ordinary obedience. It is not exalted, it is not flashy, and it is not designed to make you look or feel good about yourself.

The discipline of petitionary prayer is the school of Christian faithfulness. It is training. Chinese military strategist Sun Tzu is reported to have said that in times of peace one should prepare for war. As Christians, our preparation is prayer. And as the army that fails to train will lose its battles, so the Christian who fails to pray will falter in his or her faith. Prayer is ordinary practice for extraordinary times, and the ordinary mandate to pray in petitions is a founding principle for a faithful life.

I suspect it is the very ordinariness of prayer that makes people balk at obeying God's command. We value success but not the work that leads to success. We watch, enrapt, the Olympic events but ignore the years of training that led up to them. We gaze admiringly at great faith in others but recoil from the simple and ordinary obedience that is asked of us in prayer.

And petitionary prayer *is* very ordinary. It is the spiritual equivalent of brushing our teeth—an action we perform each day whether we like it or not, with diligence and faithfulness. And in its daily ordinariness prayer plods. It is unglamorous and mundane. It marks the daily grind of our faith. Petitionary prayer is not festal but everyday. We do not eat steak or lobster every day, but subsist most days on simpler fare—on bread or rice. Petitionary prayers are the bread-prayers of our faith.

Such bread-prayers, in all their simplistic ordinariness, are a further put-off for some people, because in the crudest interpretation petitionary prayer really is "asking God for things"—asking Him for the daily, simple, ordinary stuff of life. Prayer is not, as some of us have believed, reserved for the "big things"—as if we have a certain amount of credit with God that we do not want to waste on small matters. Prayer is for getting to work on time, to healing our colds, to finding our cars in parking lots, to helping us with assignments, to helping us make payments on cars, to helping us get different jobs, to getting guidance, to healing the sick, and beyond even these.

11

Furthermore, ordinary prayer is not just asking God once a day, but all day and every day. It is in light of this that I have finally come to terms with Paul's command to "pray continually." Rather than focusing on the impossibility of the command, or attempting to fulfill it by appealing to alternate kinds of prayer, I now believe it really means that we ought always and in every circumstance to commit each action, worry, concern, joy, and matter—no matter how infinitesimal or massive—to God in prayer.

Petitionary prayer thus imposes upon us this question: Will you trust God with the small things of your life? Will you give over to God the details of your life? Do you honestly believe you can follow God effectively when things become difficult if you are not following Him in a practical, ordinary way now? The Christian God is God of the mundane as well as the exalted. For Him, to raise the dead is as simple a matter as finding a lost set of keys. The power is not the problem; we are the problem. And the test of faith in prayer is the daily test where we are asked to trust God with what He has given us for that day—to pray, in faith, over every matter of our lives.

In all this I am reminded of the story of Naaman from 2 Kings 5, who stood before Elisha's servant and balked at dipping his body in the lowly Jordan River. His pride—"are not the rivers of my own land greater?"—stood between him and healing. But the words of his humble servants penetrated his pride, pointing to the greater truth: "If the prophet had told you to do some great thing, would you not have done it? How much more, then, when he tells you 'Wash and be cleansed'! " (2 Kings 5:13 NIV). In other words, "you are willing to do the big—why shouldn't you obey when he asks for something so small?" Humbling himself and becoming obedient to the wisdom of his servants, Naaman chose the small obedience and was healed of his leprosy. So also us, because what really keeps us from experiencing the power of God is the poverty of our obedience and the pride which thinks such things too small for us. Instead, it is in ordinary prayer that extraordinary Christians are made. It is in the small, repeated acts of obedience that we cultivate hearts that are faithful.

Questions for Group Discussion

Take a moment to consider your own prayer life. What kinds of things keep you from praying?

Do you have any particular reservations about praying in petitions? Why do you think you have those reservations?

Take a moment now and pray about your prayer life. In particular, go through your reservations and offer each one of them to God.

II

PRAYER AND POWER

Understanding Petitionary Prayer

Early on in our church prayer meetings, while I was still attempting to teach some of the basics of prayer to our group, a man we'll call Thomas came. Thomas has two great loves in life—working out and tattoos—and the result of these twin passions is a muscular and painted human being. At the end of my talk I asked if anyone had any questions or concerns, and Thomas had one: "I'm not sure," he observed, "that I understand the purpose of prayer." I remember thinking to myself, and then saying out loud, "That's a *really* good question." It was a good question—perhaps the central question of petitionary prayer. And it was a question to which I did not know the answer.

Thomas's casual but sincere comment had crystallized for me a lurking question behind petitionary prayer: If God is all-knowing, then why do we have to *ask* Him? Doesn't His omniscience make our requests redundant? Jesus himself makes this point explicit, "And when you pray, do not keep on babbling like pagans, for they think they will be heard because of their many words. Do not be like them, for your Father knows what you need before you ask him" (Matthew 6:7-8 NIV). Really? Our Father knows what we need before we ask? "Then *why*," I want to shout, "are we commanded to ask?!"

But as I looked at Thomas, with his muscular and tattooed arms, an answer occurred to me: here was a person who bore in his body the hallmarks of strength. Here was a man who had worked out and painted his body so that he could present an appearance of power, and power is what prayer is really all about. Except that prayer's power is opposite and inverted; in petitionary prayer, rather than seizing power for ourselves, we relinquish to God the control over the events, circumstances, and details of our lives. Prayer is like a spiritual workout where we practice surrendering power; one in which we flex by kneeling. Thus, the heartbeat of petitionary prayer is not control, but surrender, and that, ultimately, is why it is so difficult. And why it is so uncommon. And why it is so ordinary.

This, then, is the essence of petitionary prayer: it is the daily, hourly, moment-by-moment act where the Christian surrenders control of his or her life to God. And this deceptively simple action is the lynchpin of the great power struggle in our lives, because humans love to be in control.

Many of us are too busy controlling our lives to be bothered by God. We are too content managing our own affairs to ask Him what He thinks. And we are, perhaps, too afraid of what He might say if we did. As a result, most of us (I suspect) treat God like we treat insurance: you purchase a policy, pay your dues, and forget about it until you need to make a claim. In fact, when there is no claim you don't want to think about it at all. However, when an emergency arises and you need the agency's help you expect them to be efficient and thorough in their response. So also our relationship with God. We join our church (the policy), pay our occasional dues (going to church and [sometimes] putting money in the offering), and generally ignore God the rest of the time. We ignore Him, that is, until we need to make a claim. Some emergency comes up and suddenly we feel that we have the right to demand that He act on our behalf immediately and thoroughly. We treat God like a cosmic insurance organization and engage with Him as if He were an inconvenience. And we do this because when He is like insurance we are in control, and we prefer to control our own lives.

To be fair, trusting God is an unnatural action to fallen human beings. It is our natural (sinful) state where we seek to control our own lives without God's influence. "I'll get along fine," we think to ourselves, "without *You* interfering." We believe, wrongly, that we are fully capable of controlling our own lives. But it is precisely the do-it-ourselves attitude of humanity that is most responsible for our sin and suffering. Like inept handymen, we toss aside the instructions, refusing to ask for help, and then hammer mindlessly through our problems. Pride—belief in our own self-sufficiency—is the source of our foolishness, and at the heart of the human experience is a struggle for control between the Creator God and the prideful self.

The Genesis account of the Garden of Eden documents the beginning of this struggle. There the Serpent's temptation was for Eve to take control of her future, to be a master of her fate, rather than a servant of God's design. "You will be like God," it claimed, "knowing good and evil" (Genesis 3:5 NIV). And in taking the forbidden fruit, Eve (and Adam, too, by commiseration) took control of her life. What followed—sin— was the terrible consequence of human self-control over our lives.

While pride is the primary reason why humans reject petitionary prayer, there is a deceptively insidious counterpart to it. Perhaps you have heard someone say, regarding a prayer request, that "God's too busy to worry about that. After all, He's got to run the universe!" This sentiment reflects the common but utterly false belief that humans should reserve our prayers for some hypothetical future when it "really matters." It is based on the idea that we possess a limited quantity of good will with God that we fear to exhaust unnecessarily. But the lie of this little phrase is in its false humility. We are saying, "I am too small for God's consideration. I really don't matter that much to Him." But this is a tragic insult to God. It means that we are rejecting the testimony that He sent his Son as a sacrifice on our behalf. To claim, in false humility, that the details of our lives don't matter to God is to spit in the face of His generosity. Our lives and all their attendant details are of infinite importance to God. He gave *everything* for us; why should we not offer our everything to Him in prayer?

In these matters the shape of our struggle to understand petitionary prayer is revealed. In sin humans have rejected God's design and seek to control our lives apart from Him; we embrace an attitude of "doing it on our own" that is expressed through both pride and false humility. However, and no matter how much we struggle otherwise, these efforts are vain because our lives are only right when they are surrendered to God's control. And it is in petitionary prayer that this surrendering takes place; it is in petitionary prayer that we witness the power struggle for control of the human heart.

That, then, is the reason why we are commanded to pray in petitions and the answer to Thomas's question. The purpose of petitionary prayer is to put the power back into the hands of God; to give Him control over our lives; to surrender to Him. With each petition we strike at pride ("God, I am not in control") and reject false humility ("Yes, God, these things really matter to You"). In offering to God the details of our lives we acknowledge His supreme power over the totality of our existence; that there is no matter so great or small that it stands outside the loving care of Our Father in Heaven.

BECOMING NEEDY PEOPLE

Of course, it's easy enough to talk about "surrendering power to God." Actually doing it is another matter. And if I have accurately described the heart of petitionary prayer—that is, as the divinely ordained action where humans restore to God the control over their lives seized unjustly at the Fall—then we should expect this to be among the most difficult procedures we engage in. And so we must ask, How do we go about giving power over to God? The answer, although it sounds simple, is in fact tethered to some of the deepest complexities of our human identity: the first step in pursuing a life of surrender to God in prayer, of offering to God the power over our daily lives, is to become needy people.

Reflect upon your own prayer life and you will quickly see that prayer is easiest when we are neediest. Human beings naturally, instinctively, fall back upon prayer—whether they admit it to themselves or not—when they experience travail. Struggles regularly force us to ask for help from outside of ourselves. When someone we love is sick, we pray. When strong turbulence frightens us on an airplane, we pray. When we are lost in the dark, we pray. When soldiers are caught under fire and fear for their lives, they pray. When a person grows frustrated with the circumstances of life, he is likely in anger to pray, "Why, God?"—even if he doesn't believe in God. Prayer is easiest in proportion to our felt needs, and the more we experience suffering, or even the threat of suffering, the more likely we are to pray about those needs. We ask God to relieve those needs, to change our situations, to rescue us from whatever trouble in which we find ourselves enmeshed. I suspect that "Save me!" is the most common prayer of all humanity.

This connection makes sense, because human neediness is a prerequisite to petitionary prayer. We discover, through suffering, our needs, which we then offer to God in prayer. And yet while prayer is easiest when we are neediest, I am convinced that we do not require suffering to be praying people. I am convinced that we can, as Christians, learn to be needy apart from the crises that make our needs apparent. In fact, I believe this is the very command that Jesus gives us in his First Beatitude, the words which open the Sermon on the Mount and stand as the gateway to life in the Kingdom of God.

Consider what Jesus says there in Matthew's gospel (5:3): "Blessed are the poor in spirit," Jesus proclaims, "for theirs is the kingdom of heaven." Luke's version is slightly different; there he says simply "Blessed are the poor" (Luke 6:20). This is, Jesus seems to be saying, the First Step to becoming a Kingdom Person. If you would inherit the Kingdom of Heaven, you must become poor (in spirit). It's a prerequisite.

If you're like me, you've wondered about the differences between these phrases. Why does Matthew have one version and Luke another? The simplest explanation—that Jesus preached this sermon more than once and used different words on different occasions—doesn't help us to understand whether it is merely the poor (the objectively lowly, the materially impoverished, outcasts) or the poor "in spirit" that are blessed. It will help us if we remember that not all of Jesus' followers were poor. Some of them were quite wealthy, like Joseph of Arimathea and the women who supported Jesus' ministry out of their own wealth (Luke 8:1-3). And perhaps it was for this reason that Matthew's Beatitude contains the qualification "in spirit"—to help clarify for us that poverty, in itself, is not what Jesus is talking about when he blesses the poor. Therefore, rather than conflicting with one another, I believe that these differing beatitudes imply that there is a property common, but not exclusive to, the poor, to which Jesus is referring.

To get at this property, I reflected on what it means to be poor. I considered the opposite of poverty—riches—and what the implications of riches were for the Kingdom of God. I realized that a rich person can pretend to be contented with his things. He can believe (wrongly, I might add) that all his needs are met and that he is self-sufficient. The rich person can afford to live alone in a private home (rather than an apartment complex), and drive a car (avoiding public transit). The rich person can go through life never really needing to ask God for anything, and as a result such a person will struggle especially to realize that he is not in control of his life. The more wealth a person has, the greater the temptation to trust in that wealth. I suspect that this is exactly the reason why Jesus claims that it is no more possible for the rich to enter into the kingdom of heaven than for a camel to pass through a needle's eye.

Contrasting the rich and the poor brought Jesus' beatitude into sharp focus for me, because poverty forces humans to turn to others for help. Where the wealth of the rich can act as an isolating shell against the world, the poor are forced into community; they cannot forget their fellow souls who walk the halls of their housing and sit with them on public transit. Where the rich can trust in their own wealth, the poor know, intimately and profoundly, that they will not survive without help. The rich man can rely on himself; the poor must rely on someone else. And inasmuch as the poor understand keenly that they lack the power to meet their own needs, so the "blessed" poor recognize that they do not have any control over their lives whatsoever. Self-aware in their need, they turn to God for help. And thus, Jesus points to the poor because in poverty we see clearly what is true for all humans, rich and poor alike: our absolute need for God.

The subtlety of Jesus' teaching jolts me. No one can inherit the Kingdom of Heaven, he claims, who chooses to do it on his own. No one has a place in God's Kingdom who is in control of his own life through "riches." Mammon, in short, will sink us thoroughly. C.S. Lewis speaks to this reality when, writing as the demon Screwtape, he says that "Prosperity knits a man to the World. He feels that he is 'finding his place in it,' while really it is finding its place in him."* The more that wealth knits a person to the world and the worries of the world, the less he can take part in the Kingdom of Heaven. Hence it is the poor—the needy—who are blessed and inherit the Kingdom of God. "Blessed," Jesus is saying, "are the people who ask for help, who need God, and who realize that they cannot make it on their own, for theirs is the Kingdom of Heaven." Poverty of spirit is an indication of our neediness before God. Blessed, in other words, are the needy.

It is this language of "poor" and "poor in spirit" that provides a way to explain how we can be needy apart from the crises of neediness. If we understand that there is a characteristic of poverty which is independent of material wealth, then we can deduce that there is a characteristic of need that is independent of individual crises. This is a spirit of neediness—a spirit of fundamental dependence on God—that we must, as God's people, cultivate. It sets the stage for our prayer lives. In short, if we desire to experience God's power in our lives, then we must be fundamentally needy for His power.

This very lesson plays out in the history of Israel. In Exodus, God's people are brought out of Egypt, where suffering had made them cry out to God in neediness. He meets their needs in profound and miraculous ways—the plagues, the crossing of the sea, manna and quail in the wilderness, and water from rocks. They are provided for at every turn. But in Deuteronomy, Moses, looking ahead to when the Israelites would claim the land God had promised them, pronounces to them this warning:

---

* C.S. Lewis, *The Screwtape Letters*, letter xxviii.

But that is the time to be careful! *Beware that in your plenty you do not forget the* LORD *your God* and disobey his commands, regulations and decrees that I am giving you today. For when you have become full and prosperous and have built fine homes to live in, and when your flocks and herds have become very large and your silver and gold have multiplied along with everything else, be careful! Do not become proud at that time and forget the LORD your God, who rescued you from slavery in the land of Egypt. Do not forget that he led you through the great and terrifying wilderness with its poisonous snakes and scorpions, where it was so hot and dry. He gave you water from the rock! He fed you with manna in the wilderness, a food unknown to your ancestors. He did this to humble you and test you for your own good. *He did all this so you would never say to yourself, 'I have achieved this wealth with my own strength and energy.'* Remember the LORD your God. He is the one who gives you power to be successful, in order to fulfill the covenant he confirmed to your ancestors with an oath. (Deut 8:11-18, NLT, italics mine)

Those words in verse 8, "beware that in your plenty you do not forget the LORD," stand out to me as if in bold print, because this seems to be the great danger of our spiritual lives: that we become complacent and fat because we are comfortable; that we begin to think that our own hands and our own power have accomplished the good in our lives; that we are in control; that we forget our neediness before God. Because the more we are in control of our lives, the less God can be in control.

From this point on the story of Israel reads like a tragedy. The refrain of the book of Judges is that Israel disobeyed God (i.e., forgot Him), pursued the idols of the nations (objects of power to control our world independent of God), and were handed over to the Amalekites, Philistines, and Moabites by God as punishment for their apostasy. In each episode Israel had forgotten her *need* for God, and so God brings her to a crisis—punishment at the hands of her enemies—as a way to remind Israel of her real needs. The crisis comes, and Israel returns to the Lord in prayer, crying out for His help. In her plenty she forgot her need for God, and so God removed the plenty.

Still, there must be a way for us to achieve an attitude of neediness independent from the crises that prompt neediness. We must depend on God whether or not the Philistines are oppressing us; we must depend on Him whether or not we have food in our pantries, or money in our bank accounts, or children in our nurseries, or jobs on the horizon, in sickness and in health, for better or for worse. Because if our relationship with God always depends on a felt crisis to be real, then whenever the crisis fades so too will our relationship. We will be no better than the Israelites who in their plenty forgot their need for God. Therefore, cultivating neediness is a way to pursue God all the time, not just when something is wrong; it is to reject the mindset where God is like insurance—best invisible until needed—and embrace Him instead as a loving Father, eager to meet us in our neediness.

CULTIVATING NEEDINESS

How, then, do we create need? More importantly, how do we cultivate this spirit of neediness apart from the crises that trigger neediness? There are several things we can do. In the first place, we must become aware of our need for neediness, which is what this chapter has sought to do so far. Then, from within this understanding, we must become especially aware of the neediness that is independent of crises.

Since this may be a novel concept, a simple exercise can get us underway—a process involving memory. Because we all know the experience of need—whether rich or poor—each soul can remember that experience and what prayer was like during the period of neediness. For example, right after my wife and I began dating during university we had a bad summer breakup. It was especially bad because I was visiting her in Texas at the time, and breaking up meant a seventeen-hour drive, alone, from Dallas back to Chicago. In my need and pain I did a great deal of praying as the long, slow, flat miles passed. Today, even though the pain is gone, the memory of that need remains strong. As a result, I can now rely on my memory to help me re-enter the need, without the accompanying crisis. In short, I can apply the memory to my present prayers in order to practice neediness (without requiring another breakup!).

Think of a time of need in your own life. Remember the circumstances that brought about the need, and now, in your mind, separate the neediness from the circumstances (which, technically, you have already done since you are no longer in those circumstances). Take that spirit of neediness and apply it now to your present prayers. Remember that although your circumstances may have changed, you need God's power every bit as much right now as you did in that time of crisis. In this way you can begin to apply the spirit of neediness to your everyday life.

While remembering our need is useful and assists us to distinguish between our neediness and the crisis that occasions it, we can also actively create need through fasting. In fact, we might call fasting the spiritual discipline of neediness. In fasting, we intentionally deprive ourselves of something good to remind our souls that, in the words of Jesus and Moses, "Man does not live by bread alone" (Matt 4:4, Deut 8:3). Fasting is the creation of a temporary need in our lives in order to assist us in prayer. We abstain from food so that we can feel the need for God in our stomachs.

Of course, you can fast from more than just food (although food is the easiest and most common fast). Any place where you can deprive yourself of a good for the sake of cultivating neediness for God in your heart is a fast, and that might mean fasting from your car and taking transit for a time, or fasting from television, or fasting from social media. Note, however, that one never fasts from sinning—if it's not something you can otherwise celebrate, you shouldn't be doing it anyway.

If you're planning to fast, examine your life and choose some area to declare your dependence upon and need for God for a set period of time (for example, Lent). Set clear rules for your fast. If you choose to skip desserts for a month, does that include sugar in your coffee? Do you make an exception for your son's birthday party? Clear rules will help you to keep the fast. Furthermore, always choose a fast that you can reasonably accomplish. Don't set out to pray 23 hours a day, eating only one meal consisting of a slice of dry bread and a thimbleful of water. Such a fast will teach you not a lesson about need, but failure.

Self-deprivation like this is not instinctual; it goes against the grain of our nature. Yet this experience is essential to our spiritual development. Years ago when I first began to observe Lent I determined to skip my lunch on each of Lent's six Fridays. Since my workplace had a common lunch room and I wanted to avoid questions about why I wasn't eating, I would get in my car and drive to a nearby parking lot. There I would read my Bible and listen to worship music. I quickly discovered on that first Friday that parking near a Wendy's and smelling the grill was not the best choice of location. Despite even the smells, those first Fridays were terrible. I was a cranky and miserable person the following afternoon. I snapped at my wife when I got home that night. However, by the third week something changed in me. My time of devotion in the car began to become powerful and sweet—and for the following weeks I actually looked forward to skipping lunch on Fridays! The simple act of depriving myself of one meal a week, of humbling myself in a fast, created the need-space in my heart for God to work in my life. Rather than waiting for a crisis to call on God, I was teaching my soul that it needed God all the time.

There is a third way to grow a spirit of neediness, and unlike memory and fasting, which we must actively pursue, this path to neediness is passively present in the life of every human being. This path is anxiety, and learning to attend to and harness its energy is a powerful way to cultivate neediness.

The simplest definition of anxiety is that it is a fear of the unknown. More than merely fear, however, anxiety is a persistent worrying about that unknown—an attempt, through worry, to control the uncontrollable. Anxiety is a manifestation of our need for security and control over those things in our lives over which we have no control. We worry about our children's futures, about the day of our death, about the debt we cannot shake. Anxiety betrays the desperate neediness of the human heart for control; yet ironically the more control we attempt, the greater our anxiety will be. This is because the control we need is not our own, but God's, and as pangs of hunger tell us we need food, anxiety tells us that we need God.

Anxiety is differentiated from common fear, observes theologian Helmut Thielicke, because "As long as I am simply afraid, that is, as long as I fear something definite, I continue to have hope as well. I fear I have cancer, but maybe it is only a harmless swelling, or maybe there is an unexpected possibility of a cure."* Anxiety, by contrast, moves beyond the definite— that which we know—into the unknown and unknowable. Of course, the unknown is the most obvious of those things over which we have no control; take, for example, that mysterious thing called *tomorrow*, about which many people worry, and over which no one has power. Inasmuch, then, as we have only limited power over the knowable, it follows that we have absolutely no power over the *un*knowable. Therefore the experience of anxiety is precisely what one would expect for a humanity that has overstepped the bounds of its relationship with God. God alone is in control of all the unknowables of human existence—of our living and dying, of our families and fortunes, of all our tomorrows—and when we attempt to control that which God alone is fit to control, anxiety is the natural consequence.

---

* Helmut Thielicke, *Being a Christian When the Chips are Down* (Philadelphia: Fortress, 1977), 25.

When God is in control—when He is for us a loving and caring Father—then there is no need for anxiety. But when we have rejected both Him and His gifts, then every circumstance becomes an opportunity for fear. Thus, anxiety is not limited to those great uncontrollable fears (when we will die, what will happen in 20 years), but stretches all the way down to our daily lives—to every place, in fact, where we attempt to keep control rather than giving it to God. Anxiety reigns when we seize control of our relationships, of our promotions, of our families, of the stoplights that keep us from getting to work on time, of, indeed, every tiny detail of our lives. And the more we seek to control our existences, the more anxiety we will experience because anxiety is cumulative. It is also paralyzing. Linguistically, anxiety is linked to the concept of choking, and the experience of anxiety is very much like ropes that creep up and coil around our arms and necks. Anxiety is the internal equivalent of running on a treadmill with the hopes of travelling from our home to the park; all our desperate effort gets us nowhere, and we are exhausted at the end. Worry, when it does not drive us to God, is an utter and paralyzing waste of energy.

This is precisely what Jesus means when he makes the following statement near the conclusion of his Sermon on the Mount:

Therefore I tell you, do not worry [*lit. be not anxious*] about your life, what you will eat or drink; or about your body, what you will wear. Is not life more important than food, and the body more important than clothes?... Who of you by worrying can add a single hour to his life?... So do not worry, saying "What shall we eat?" or "What shall we drink?" or "What shall we wear?" For the pagans run after all these things, and your heavenly Father knows that you need them. But seek first his kingdom and his righteousness, and all these things will be given to you as well. Therefore do not worry about tomorrow, for tomorrow will worry about itself. Each day has enough trouble of its own. (Matt 6:25, 27, 31-34 NIV)

In this passage Jesus is not advocating irresponsibility; rather, he wants us to place greater trust in God. Worry, he knows, is the sign that we are attempting to control our lives, and its absence is the sign that we have given that control to God. Therefore do not be anxious, Jesus commands, about even the most basic details of your life—eating, drinking, clothing. God knows our needs, God is sufficient to meet our needs, and therefore we ought to seek His Kingdom and righteousness first. When we do this we are placing our trust in Him; in short, we are *needing* Him, and He Himself will provide for our needs.

Anxiety is thus the mechanism that shows us we have overstepped the bounds of control in our lives. If we can learn to place a finger on the pulse of our anxiety it will serve as a constant reminder of our need for God. Seen this way, each experience of anxiety is an opportunity to express our need for God—even more, it is an opportunity for God to meet our needs. Every experience of anxiety is a prompt to pray.

Once we have become aware of our anxiety, how do we turn it into a sense of need for God? How do we practically move from the experience of worry to the expression of need? The simple answer is that we have to offer—to surrender—our worry to God in prayer. We have to acknowledge our concern, our fear, that place we have been attempting to control through worry, and make a conscious choice to hand it over to God in an act of surrender. This offering cannot be an on-the-fly, slapped-together prayer. To truly offer our anxiety to God will require a dedicated time of stillness. If we reject stillness, then our prayers will merely become an extension of our worry—we will pray to control our reality rather than surrendering our reality to God in prayer.

Two simple things have helped me accomplish this process. The first is to kneel. We must get upon our knees in a posture of humble submission before Almighty God. This is because prayer is not merely a function of our minds but includes our bodies as well. In the same way, anxiety is something we don't merely think but something we feel—it sits in our bellies like a bad lunch—and therefore the best way to combat the power of anxiety over our hearts is to humbly submit our bodies to God. Once we have knelt, our perspective of the universe will pivot; having bent our knees in surrender, we will begin to see things God's way. This is because it is never from the "higher" viewpoint of control that things make sense, but only from the "lower" viewpoint of surrender.

The second thing that helps me to give over my anxieties to God is to hold my hands in a posture of offering—cupping them before me. In that position, I am imaginatively handing the worrisome detail of my life over to God, once again cementing a spiritual reality with a physical gesture.

When I was in seminary I applied for a job grading assignments for a professor. But after I had applied I grew worried. Was I qualified? Was I capable of doing this kind of work? Was it going to be too much for me to do in the term? A host of questions crowded in upon me and began to choke me; I began to regret having applied for the job at all. But in the midst of my anxiety God broke through and reminded me that He was the one in control, that I could not, by worry, change the situation. Beginning to accept God's perspective on the matter, I got down on my knees in my office, held out my hands in front of me, and prayed: "God, if you want me to take this job, please have the professor offer it to me. If not, please give it to someone else." Immediately a sense of peace washed over me, and I knew that God had heard my prayer. I moved from trying to control my circumstances to trusting God to be *in control* of my circumstances. This is how I believe anxiety ought to function in the Christian life: as a cattle-prod toward prayer. (As it turned out, the professor offered me the job, and I took it with confidence that God had led me to it.)

I suspect that if you have done any praying in your life, this process will not be unfamiliar to you—anxiety, followed by prayer, followed by peace, and then an answer. The peace of God always follows the pressure of anxiety, and we always know when we have successfully offered our worries over to Him by the peace and sense of God's control that washes over us.

At this point I want to offer an important caveat: anxiety for some people is magnified by a medical condition, a bio-chemical imbalance in their bodies. For such a person, the last thing he or she needs is the bad spiritual advice to "just pray more." Such advice will only amplify the believer's anxiety, and can eventually lead to despair that this person isn't "doing enough" or "getting it right." Instead, he or she needs the help of a physician and possibly medication. Once the physical condition that creates the anxiety is addressed, that person will be able to attend to its call to prayer in a healthy way.

THE NEED FOR REPETITION

So far in this chapter we have observed that prayer is where we return power over our lives to God, that we must begin by becoming needy, and that we become needy as we remember, fast, and attend to our anxiety. Each of these, considered together, illuminate the reason why the Christian must "pray continually." We pray continually because we are continually seizing control; we are always seizing power; we are always experiencing anxiety, and we are always forgetting our fundamental neediness before God. This is the primary answer to the question (troubling to many) of why we must pray in repetition. Because if prayer is the field upon which the battle for control of the human soul is fought, then our need to pray repeatedly should not surprise us. Sin works actively in our lives against our daily surrender to God; we release the day's anxieties to God, only to take them up again the next day, or the next hour, or even the next minute. And every time we discover that we have taken control we must return that control to God in prayer. Our sin demands repetition in prayer. And the dynamic process of surrendering power to God through cultivated neediness is one that we must perform at all times. We must pray continually.

Still, some might feel that the need to pray in repetition involves a kind of capriciousness on God's part—after all, if He is all-powerful and all-knowing, then why does He need me to ask Him for things repeatedly? It is important to remember that we do not pray to give God information; as Jesus said (notably twice at both Matthew 6:8 and 6:32), our Father already knows our needs. And we are not to babble when we pray—that is the way of the nations who think that many words are necessary to

34

ensure that their request is heard. Petitionary prayer is not about spamming God with requests, but about something that happens in our hearts. In the film *Shadowlands* C.S. Lewis, played by Anthony Hopkins, says the following about the necessity of prayer: "It doesn't change God, it changes me." And this rings true for all our experiences. We repeat our prayers not because God is deaf or negligent but because we are. The change in the balance of power has not yet been brought about.

The parable of the persistent widow in Luke 18 offers a snapshot of this process. In that parable a widow brings her request to a judge who neither fears God nor cares for man. Her persistence nets her an answer, not because the judge finally cares about her, but because he wants relief from her nagging. Jesus, in teaching this, does not mean for us to think that God is in any way like the judge. Quite the opposite, God both cares for man and honors His own character. The message of the parable, then, is that we must pray persistently to the One who both hears and cares for us, and that we must pray in repetition until we have been heard. We, like the widow, must continually, repeatedly, persistently offer our anxieties to God in prayer until the peace of God (as the sign of our being heard) enters into our hearts and our anxiety is released. Only then can we cease praying about that particular anxiety.

THE REWARD OF PRAYER

These, then, are the foundations of petitionary prayer: power, given to God through neediness, achieved through memory, fasting, and attention to anxiety, and pursued with repetition. Collectively, each of these reflects a kind of justice about petitionary prayer, because prayer is fundamentally about returning to God—in surrendering to Him control of our lives—what is His due. But in addition to its justice there is also a great reward to petitionary prayer. That reward is this: if we will cultivate hearts that are needy for God, we will experience God Himself.

This is the deeper spiritual reality to which our ordinary human needs point, and to which cultivating an attitude of neediness can direct us. Attention to our ordinary needs can open our eyes and hearts to see the need that is behind all needs—the need for God Himself. Scottish author George MacDonald, in proposing an answer to the question of why we pray in petitions, says the following:

> I answer, What if he [God] knows prayer to be the thing we need first and most? What if the main object in God's idea of prayer be the supplying of our great, our endless need— the need of himself? What if the good of all our smaller and lower needs lies in this, that they help to drive us to God? Hunger may drive the runaway child home, and he may or may not be fed at once, but he needs his mother more than his dinner. Communion with God is the one need of the soul beyond all other need; prayer is the beginning of that communion, and some need is the motive of that prayer.
>
> Our wants are for the sake of our coming into communion with God, our eternal need.[*]

---

[*] George Macdonald, *Unspoken Sermons, Series I, II, III* (Whitehorn: Johansen, 1997), 235.

In other words, every human need we experience is like a bell summoning us to the table of God; every craving in our hearts and lives an invitation to God's feast. As we grow to acknowledge and regularly respond to this need-summons, we will simultaneously come to recognize, as MacDonald says of God elsewhere, that "Every time you feel you want me, that is a sign I am wanting you."[*] At that feast, if we are obedient and attend, God will satisfy us with nothing less than Himself.

Cultivating neediness, then—which is really nothing more than the practical and ordinary business of surrendering our lives completely to God—is the first step of prayer. And yet it remains a step beyond which we never grow. It is one we will ploddingly repeat day in and day out for the rest of our lives, because it is the step that takes us on the path from our immediate human needs into communion with God. As a result, growing into spiritual maturity through prayer is a matter of seeing in every ordinary need an opportunity to experience God's great gift of Himself.

In keeping with the inverted, opposite power of petitionary prayer, prayer that moves in a direction contrary to the natural inclinations of the human heart, my church's prayer group began to pray that God would make us a needy people. This, on the surface, is an odd prayer, and one that needs explanation to new members. After all, nobody likes needy people—we often make a special point to avoid them. But the kind of neediness for which we ask is not the neediness of the world, but instead that powerlessness that will give God the space He requires to act in our lives. It is the neediness that begs for God

---

[*] George Macdonald, *The Wise Woman and Other Stories* (Grand Rapids: Eerdmans, 1980), 96.

Himself to be the answer to our prayers. We are seeking, like David in the Psalms, to have souls that thirst for the Lord "as parched land thirsts for rain" (Ps 143:6, NLT).*

As we become needy people, the character of our faith should change. For one thing, as needy people we will ask for help. We will realize that we cannot go it alone, that we must have the assistance of Almighty God to make it in life. For another, our needs will drive us to community—in particular, God's special community, the Church. In fact, it is from within such needy, petitionary prayers that we *become* the Church for one another.

What is more, as we become needy people we will have eyes and ears that open to see God's goodness. When you have lost something that matters to you, your need awakens all of your senses to attend to finding what you lost. In the same way, when our hearts are needy for God, our spiritual senses are enlivened. Consider this as well: one of the curious byproducts of losing something is that you often find all sorts of things you weren't looking for but had lost anyway. In searching for your lost keys you find a pen you missed, some loose change you wanted, and a receipt you had misplaced. In the same way, in our need for God our spiritual senses awaken and we begin to see Him more and more. Searching for Him in one area of life opens our eyes to see Him in all the areas of our lives.

Lastly, as we become needy people our eyes and ears will be opened to the neediness of others. Awareness of our own need

---

* In fact, without a theology of neediness, the Psalms become incomprehensible. They are songs that are all about needing God, remembering our need for God, and petitioning God to be Himself the answer to our need.

for God will awaken us to that need in others, and then spur us on in our commission to help them satisfy their true, deepest need.

In Revelation 3:14-22, Jesus spoke a stern message to the church at Laodicea. They thought themselves rich and finely clothed, and did not realize their poverty, nakedness, and blindness. In their plenty, they had forgotten their need for God. In the place of their outward wealth Jesus commanded them to buy clothes and gold and eye salve from him; to become needy toward Jesus. This is the inverted, opposite power of the Kingdom of God—the self-surrendering power of people who choose need over self-sufficiency, poverty of spirit over the riches of the world. This is the power which Paul claims in 2 Corinthians 12:7-10, the power of God which "is made perfect in weakness"—power which shows up best in, showcases itself in, is only truly visible in, the weaknesses of humans. Not that we pursue or value weakness as an end in itself, but recognize rather that the gaps, the areas of need in our lives, are the places where God is most able to perform His wonders. The reward for the Laodiceans, and us, is nothing less than the gift of God Himself.

Questions for Group Discussion

Have you experienced a time of need when prayer was easy?

Have you experienced anxiety, followed by prayer, followed by peace? Tell the story.

Can you think of some ways to personally connect your daily needs—food, fellowship, work, rest—to your deepest need for God?

Have you ever fasted? What was the experience like?

III

Postures of Prayer
How to Pray

Most people who have attended church have been exposed to ministers and laity who, while relatively easy to talk to in normal conversation, adopt strange ways of speaking when they pray. Otherwise sensible people speak to God in code as if He only understood King James English: "Thou O Lord art most Holy and Wise and to Thee we give thanks for Thy bountiful care this day." Or, using familiar words, people adopt strange intonations—almost as if they were chanting incantations—booming and hushing at odd and unpredictable moments: "O LORD we THANK you for all your GOODness and MERcy." Sometimes the prayers are constructed entirely in "Christianese"—churchy language that is largely incomprehensible to the uninitiated: "Lord, you predestined us to be your elect people, and through the propitiation of Christ have made substitution for our iniquity."

There is no question that these people are very serious about their prayers. And yet it seems to me that rather than talking to God these Christians are doing something different. Rather than praying, they are posturing.

Posturing in prayer happens when we awkwardly contort our language so that we can appear a certain way; we bend and twist our words so that people will think about us in the way we want them to. We find a clear picture of this posturing in the first conversation between Adam, Eve, and God after the Fall. There, instead of talking with God, those humans were focused on trying to make themselves look good. Consequently, they contorted themselves into all sorts of different poses during that conversation: Adam pointed at Eve, Eve pointed at the snake, both of them pointed at God, and all the while they looked ridiculous dressed in fig leaves. God, of course, was not fooled for a moment. In a similar way, using special language in prayer can make us appear wise and knowledgeable, but ultimately when we try on ancient words, or theological terms, or bizarre intonations, I suspect that we look just as ridiculous as Adam and Eve did—equally absurd, and equally easy for God to see through.

In some ways this posturing is understandable, because adopting foreign vocabulary and bizarre intonation is one way to mitigate some of the difficulties of ordinary prayer. When we hold fake and formal conversations with a person we guarantee a level of distance between us; controlled language is employed to control a relationship. This, again, is what we see with Adam and Eve, who hedge and hide because they are afraid to disclose themselves fully to God. In the same way, formal prayers can become protections against intimacy with God.

Posturing in prayer also happens when people believe that God only hears prayers done "a certain way." Such people feel, implicitly and because of the example of their leaders (whom they are dutifully following), that we require special words to approach God. And so, rather than talking to God as they are, they learn the "code" of the church. After all, they reason, He's God, and aren't there protocols for speaking with Supreme Beings? If we don't observe them will God really hear us? If we fail to keep them won't our requests be lost in the paperwork like improperly worded letters to a bureaucratic organization?

There is no doubt that God is gracious and continues to hear all these prayers (whether or not we understand them), and yet such posturing is starkly opposed to the ordinariness of prayer. The more specialized prayer becomes—the more it is locked into certain forms and traditions—the further it is removed from the grasp of the ordinary believers who are commanded to do it. As a result, people balk when you ask them to pray—whether privately, in a small group, or before the church. They are afraid that they don't know how; afraid that they'll use the wrong words or say the wrong things; that they don't know the language of prayer. Posturing in prayer has made such a deep impression into people's minds that it is difficult to communicate to them that there are no right words for prayer—only right attitudes; that making right prayers to God is not a matter of intonation, or special words, or a special language. It is difficult to communicate to people that God doesn't care how sonorous your voice is, how eloquent you are, how wise you appear, or how theologically accurate your prayer is. He doesn't care if you stutter, or start only to come to a standstill, or forget what you were saying, or pray in sentence fragments. Ordinary prayer is for ordinary people who use ordinary language. Because when it comes right down to it, the particular words you use in prayer are irrelevant; it is your attitude in prayer that matters to Him.

This chapter, then, is about how to pray. But since the specific words of prayer are irrelevant, I will focus instead on our attitudes in prayer—what I call our posture in prayer. In contrast to *posturing*, where we contort ourselves to appear certain ways, our *posture* before God deals with standing upright before Him. Our desire is to have right posture before our God—not to posture ourselves. And it is to three such postures that I want to speak now: humility, confidence, and boldness.

HUMILITY

The first posture of prayer is humility, and humility is a deeply rooted, inner attitude of honesty about ourselves in the light of Who God is. What this means in practice is that when we approach God in prayer we should approach Him as we are, the people that we really are, broken and sad, happy and contented, in whatever circumstances we find ourselves at that moment. In prayer, observes theologian Helmut Thielicke, "I need only be fully who I am right now."* Therefore when we present ourselves in prayer we must do it humbly to the God who sees all and knows all. Posturing—pretending to be other than we are—is out of the question.

---

* Helmut Thielicke, *Being a Christian When the Chips are Down* (Philadelphia: Fortress, 1977), 51.

In Luke 18 Jesus tells a story about two men who went to the temple to pray. One was a Pharisee (a religious professional) and the other was a tax collector (a social and religious outcast). The Pharisee, Jesus says, stood on his own and prayed the following, "God, I thank you that I am not like the rest of men, swindlers, the unrighteous, adulterers, or even as this tax collector. I fast twice between Sabbaths and I give a tenth of all I get" (18:11-12, author's translation). This Pharisee is praying for the benefit, not of his relationship with God, but for himself. He is praying so that others can hear—so that the tax collector can hear—and in the end the primary recipient of his prayer is himself, which is a point some manuscripts make explicit when they contain the phrase: "he stood on his own *and prayed to himself.*"

In the best case scenario our Pharisee is merely confused. He is praying in the only way he knows how. He is praying as he learned to pray from all the other Pharisees at Pharisee school. But at worst (and this appears to be Jesus' intention), he is posturing himself to look good while praying. And what is wicked about his prayer is that all his exalted language is, in truth, geared to derive a sense of self-worth at the tax collector's expense. The whole prayer marks the Pharisee's refusal to acknowledge his own need before God.

The Pharisee exhibits an important lesson for us, and that is that the opposite of humility is not pride, but pretence. We are most often not humble, not because we are prideful, but because we are pretending to be something we are not. And there is a natural confusion between these concepts because sinful pride is what generates pretence.

Pride, in its biblical sense, is a synonym for confidence. What that means is that confidence (also called "boasting") is neutral; it is neither good nor bad, but it can be properly or improperly placed. We can trust (take pride, express confidence) in proper things or we can trust in improper things. "Some trust in chariots, and some in horses," says the psalmist, pointing to places of improper trust—"but we," he concludes, pointing to the right basis for confidence, "trust in the name of the LORD our God" (Psalm 20:7 NIV). It is in this sense that pride is labeled as the sin of the Garden of Eden. There, Adam and Eve took their confidence and placed it upon themselves, rather than God. Another clear picture of this false confidence can be seen in both First and Second Corinthians. In those letters Paul rebukes a church that was "prideful" because they were boasting (that is, trusting, placing confidence, exhibiting pride) in their status—whether their apostle, their spiritual gifts, their talents, or otherwise—when they should have been trusting only in Christ. And thus the "pride" of our Pharisee is that he places confidence in his own righteousness—a point Jesus makes explicit in verse 9: "He spoke this parable to some who *believed in themselves* that they were righteous" (italics mine).

Misplaced confidence—that is, sinful pride—gives birth to pretence. (Here I should note that the language of "pretence," "posturing," and "pretending" all speak to the same reality.) The reason for this is simple: once we have believed a fundamental falsehood about ourselves we begin to pretend to be other than we are; we twist our personalities to match our false foundations. In practice this can range from the ridiculous to the wicked. On the ridiculous side, a man on a date with a girl he likes may, thinking he needs to behave a certain way for her to like him (belief in a falsehood), say all sorts of things he doesn't mean (pretence, or posturing). A woman, believing (falsely) that she is inadequate for a certain job will lie on her résumé (pretence). More seriously, a person who believes (falsely) that God only hears prayers done a "certain way" may pray in church with affected words and mannerisms (pretence). Even more seriously, believing (falsely) that God doesn't really care or notice how we behave, we engage in the pretence of sin (and sin, in the end, is a profound contortion—a twisting—of our true nature). Lastly, to offer a severe biblical example, when national Israel was faced with the threat of the vast, invading Babylonian armies, they trusted in their temple rather than the God of the temple (Jeremiah 7:4). From that false confidence they came to act pretentiously as if their nation could not and would not be conquered. They were, of course, catastrophically wrong. In each case what has happened is that by placing trust in things which are improper, our personalities adapt to match our false beliefs. This process in part informs God's pronouncement upon Israel that, "having eyes they will not see and ears they will not hear."* When we trust in a thing that is not God— which is idolatry—we become like the thing that we trust; trusting in idols which are blind and deaf, we inevitably become as blind and deaf as our idols. Hence, belief in a lie (idolatry, false confidence) produces inevitable consequences in our personalities (pretence).

The Pharisee exhibits this process clearly. Believing (falsely) that he is righteous—that is, placing false confidence in his own works—he pretends to be other than he is. He engages in pretence. He neglects, or avoids, or just has no concept whatso-

---

* See, for example, Psalm 115:6, Isaiah 6:10, Jeremiah 5:21, et al.

ever of how God views him, and as a result his approach to God is marked by a fundamental dishonesty within himself; a dishonesty that is rooted in his ignorance of God's perfect knowledge and holiness. In the prayer of this Pharisee we have a clear picture of the pretence that is the opposite of humility.

The tax collector is the foil to the Pharisee's pretence. He does not stand. He is not at the centre, but far off. He does not lift his eyes to heaven. He beats his breast (a sign of repentance) and prays, "God, be merciful to me, a sinner." His actions and prayer are meant for God; he is not playing for a human audience. In the end, when Jesus pronounces his firm judgment on these two figures, only one of them left the temple justified, and this is because "all who exalt themselves will be humbled, but the one who humbles himself will be exalted" (Luke 18:14, author's translation).

It is the humility—indeed, the active self-humbling—of the tax collector that makes his prayer effective. And it is important to stress that he was not heard because he used special actions or special words; there is nothing magic about beating one's breast or the words, "Be merciful to me, a sinner." These things are the outward expressions of an inward reality, and it is that inward reality that we must seek to imitate in our prayers. We must adopt a posture of humility.

If pretence is pretending to be other than we really are, then humility is about having a right sense of ourselves before God. It is a fundamental honesty about our lives in the light of God's revealing light. And the way to generate this true humility is by contemplating the holiness of God. Here the scriptures give us guidance. In 1 John 1:5 we read that "God is light." What this means for humility is that we must allow the light of God to shine through our lives—we must strip off the fig leaves and abandon the posturing we so love to do—and through this uncomfortable process we must allow ourselves to be exposed for who we really are. The prophet Isaiah, exposed to God's holiness in this way, exclaims that he was a sinful man who lived among a people of sinful lips (Isaiah 6); his encounter with the revealing light of God's holiness was the cause of an honest assessment of his personal sinfulness. We also read in the scriptures about God's perfect knowledge, as Psalm 139:4, 7 (NIV) testifies: "Before a word is on my tongue you know it completely, O LORD... Where can I go from your Spirit? Where can I flee from your presence? If I go up to the heavens, you are there; if I make my bed in Sheol,* you are there." There is nothing we can hide from Him and nowhere we can go where He is not. It is in this sense that David humbles himself after his sin with Bathsheba; he presents himself honestly before God and shows his awareness of God's holy knowledge when he says that "against you, you only, have I sinned and done what is evil in your sight" (Psalm 51:4 NIV). Thus, humility in prayer is a measure of our willingness to acknowledge, as we present ourselves before Him, God's perfect and holy knowledge of our imperfections. It involves a change in perspective, because exposure to God's holiness always changes how we look at our lives.

In fact, it is reflection upon the holiness and perfect knowledge of God that causes us to confess our sin. Confession literally means "to speak with"—in other words, when we confess, we are agreeing that what God sees in our lives (our sin, brokenness, and our need for Him) is true. Confession is

---

* That is, the place of the dead.

the shedding of pretence, and is a powerful doorway to humble honesty with God.

Confession ought to be the regular practice of every believer, but it comes with a subtle danger. That danger is that, out of proportion, it can make our ordinary praying a guilt-ridden and odious business—quite the opposite of what prayer ought to be. We can feel guilty for not confessing, we can obsess over confessing every detail of our lives, and in a host of ways we can, by our own anxiety, scuttle our times of prayer.

As a way out of this trap, I like to use a pre-written prayer of confession like the following one found in the *Book of Common Prayer*:

> *Most merciful God,*
> *we confess that we have sinned against you*
> *in thought, word, and deed,*
> *by what we have done,*
> *and by what we have left undone.*
> *We have not loved you with our whole heart;*
> *we have not loved our neighbors as ourselves.*
> *We are truly sorry and we humbly repent.*
> *For the sake of your Son Jesus Christ,*
> *have mercy on us and forgive us;*
> *that we may delight in your will,*
> *and walk in your ways,*
> *to the glory of your Name. Amen.*[*]

Such a prayer concisely summarizes the breadth of sin in our lives, and while there may be times when God needs us to

---

[*] *The Book of Common Prayer* (New York: Oxford University Press, 1990), 79

address particular sins in prayer with more specific care and attention, on most days a prayer such as this should be sufficient to remind us both of God's holy knowledge and our desperate need for Him.

In addition to regular confession, the very process of presenting ourselves before God in prayer to ask for something is an act of self-humbling. To ask, we must first acknowledge need, and to acknowledge need is to be aware of our deficiencies before God. What is more, to ask God for help with our needs is to acknowledge that He has what we lack. This process is cumulative, and the more we cast ourselves upon God in neediness, the more we will recognize our dependence upon Him—the humbler we will become. God's holiness reveals our need, our neediness becomes the doorway to greater humility.

Still, there remains a great deal of confusion about humility in our world, and most of this confusion stems from our misdiagnosis of pride. Thinking that pride (which, remember, is a neutral confidence) was the opposite of humility, we have wrongly identified humility with lack of confidence. As a result we are suspicious of people who take credit for things they do, and at times we even accuse confident people of being prideful. We (wrongly) identify the humble person as the one who rejects all compliments, denigrates his own work, is rarely noticed, and is profoundly timid. What is more, because humility is today considered a virtue and something to be achieved (it wasn't always), we can actually *posture* ourselves to appear humble. We actively pretend to be small, or reject praise, or avoid credit for the work we do, so that we can appear "humble" by the standard of the world, or, better yet, merely so that we won't appear "prideful." We have created a pretence of humility which is undeniably a false humility. This is precisely what we see when we consider the person who neglects prayer because he doesn't want to "bother God with the details of my life"—the pretence of a false humility. And all this is because we have come to believe that humility means self-deprecation—that the virtue of humility is primarily in humiliating yourself. We have allowed the great Christian virtue of humility to be poisoned by the concept of humiliation.

In the end, to pray with humility is synonymous with having a genuine conversation with God. We contemplate Him as He is, reflecting upon His holiness; then, having been revealed in that light as broken and needy people, speak to Him as we are. We cast aside fig leaves and seek to make ourselves genuinely present before Him. We speak to God, and God alone, and that means that, unlike the Pharisee in Jesus' story, we reject posturing in our prayers by casting off the pretences of our knowledge, status, righteousness, heritage, education, and everything else. In this way, says C.S. Lewis, "The prayer preceding all prayers is 'May it be the real I who speaks. May it be the real Thou that I speak to.'"[*] And this is the goal of our humility—the rejection of pretence and embrace of honesty before God.

Humility is an all-important first step in prayer because most of us, unawares, are more like the Pharisee than the tax collector. Humility does not come naturally to us, and we are, in our native sinful state, far more likely to pretend than be honest in our prayers. After all, this is a lesson we've learned

---

[*] C. S. Lewis, *Letters to Malcolm: Chiefly on Prayer*, letter xv.

well from Adam and Eve. And our reason for pretending is, in the same way as the Pharisee, sourced in our misplaced confidence. In its most essential form, this misplaced confidence was the subject of the previous chapter—that we seek to control our own lives by our own power. Our prayers, therefore, are pretentious because they are built upon self-confidence. Humility is thus the first posture of prayer because it is the demolishing of this false edifice—our pretence. After all, a building, no matter how elegantly constructed, is worthless if its foundation is not secure. And in this way pretence must be demolished before our real foundations can be laid. Once we have stripped away our pretence we are finally in a position to address our misplaced confidence.

CONFIDENCE IN GOD'S POWER

Confidence is the second posture of prayer, and this posture addresses the ground on which we stand. We are confident in prayer when we stand upon firm ground; we are timid when we stand on unsure ground. Confidence, to continue the metaphor, is about our footing before God.

During the frigid winters of my hometown near Chicago lakes regularly freeze over, and, as anyone who has lived in such a cold climate knows, a frozen lake is a great place to play. But the winters in Chicago, while really cold, are neither as long nor as cold as those of the more northerly neighbors in Wisconsin, Michigan and Canada. As a result, no one ever really walks on the ice with confidence. Instead, you walk timidly, straining your ears for the telltale sounds of cracking ice that signal danger. By contrast, one year I attended a winter camp in Wisconsin where the local lake had frozen solid. There, the inventive staff had attached an inner tube to a snowmobile by a length of rope. The result—being dragged across frozen ice while hanging on for dear life—was both exhilarating and unforgettable. Such an adventure, however, is only possible when one is confident that the lake is truly frozen; that it will not buckle and crack beneath the weight of the snowmobile.

When we approach God in prayer, we do not approach Him timidly or fearful of losing our footing. We do not approach Him afraid that the ground beneath us might prove unreliable. We never need approach Him with our ears strained for the sound of His impending fury. Instead, we approach God with a posture of confidence. And, in the same way that humility develops by contemplating God's holiness, so confidence is built by contemplating God's power and love. These two things are the ground—the foundation—of our confidence. We must reflect upon each of them if we would have confidence grow in our prayers.

If we continue with the image of footing, then the first "foot" of our confidence in God is to trust in His power. What I mean by this is that as we contemplate, understand, and apprehend the power of God, our posture before Him will reflect a remarkable confidence. This, I believe, is precisely what Paul prays for the Ephesian church in his first great prayer for that congregation in Ephesians 1:16-23:

> I have not stopped giving thanks for you, remembering you in all my prayers, in order that the God of our Lord Jesus Christ, the Father of glory, should give you a spirit of wisdom and revelation in the knowledge of Him—know-

ledge that would enlighten the eyes of your heart so that you might know what is the hope of His calling, what is the wealth of the glory of His inheritance among the saints, and what is the surpassing greatness of His power for we who believe. [This power is revealed] according to the working of his mighty strength which he worked in Christ, raising him from the dead and seating him at His right hand in the heavens above all rulers and authorities and powers and lordships and every name that can be named, not only in this age but in the age to come. And He [God] subjected all things under his feet and gave him the headship over all things in the Church, which is his body, the fullness of all things, in all things, being fulfilled (Ephesians 1:16-23, author's translation).

In verses 16 and 17 Paul gives thanks for the Ephesian church, then he asks that God the Father would give them wisdom and insight to enable them to know God more. The remainder of his prayer, verses 18-23, documents the kind of knowledge that Paul desires them to have. Verse 18 begins this request with the evocative petition that God would, "enlighten the eyes of your heart so that you may know." With our natural eyes we see physical things, with the eyes of our hearts we see spiritual things, and here Paul asks for spiritual enlightenment so that the Ephesians may see divine things. He then lists, in some detail, the divine things he wants them to know, which are three facets of the power of God that are invisible to the natural human eye: the hope of God's calling, the wealth of His inheritance, and His mighty strength.

First, Paul wants us to know the hope that belongs to those called by God. That hope, both in Ephesians and throughout the New Testament, is the promise of resurrection from the dead that is given to every believer in Christ. It is the assured knowledge that by the power of the Spirit of God we need not fear death. Second, Paul wants us to know the wealth of the glory of God's inheritance among the saints. The deposit, or down payment, of our inheritance is the Holy Spirit (cf. Eph 1:14). As a deposit, He is a foretaste of the inheritance to come, but as a present reality He is also the active power of God working in our world today. To know the wealth of the glory of God's inheritance is therefore to know and live as the empowered inheritors of God's Spirit that we are. Third, and most expansively, Paul wants us to know God's surpassingly great power, the description of which dominates the remainder of his prayer. It is (v19) power that is *for* those who believe—in other words, it works for and belongs to us. It is also (v19) power which is witnessed in the working of God's mighty strength, which is revealed particularly in raising Christ from the dead. Hence, this power is the resurrection power of the Spirit which, having raised Jesus, will raise us from the dead as well (cf. Rom 8:11). It is the power that seats Christ at God's right hand in heaven (v20), it has raised Christ above all imaginable earthly and heavenly powers (v21), and it has placed all things under his feet, which is an image of the complete subjection of the universe to Christ (v22). God, in short, through Christ, has accomplished His complete purpose for the universe—both in working our salvation, and in bringing to fulfillment God's great plan. Jesus Christ, the conquering King, is the one on whom we rest the full weight of our confidence.

But then comes a startling turn of phrase, because it says in verses 22 and 23 of Paul's prayer that God, by this mighty power, has given Christ headship over all things *in the Church*, which is Christ's body, "the fullness of all things, in all things, being fulfilled." In other words, this mighty power, which Paul is eager for you to know, is *your* power in Christ Jesus. That you, having the Spirit of God through your baptism, are going to be resurrected with Christ (this is both our wealth and our hope). That you, as the Church, as the body of Jesus Christ, are seated on the throne with God above all earthly powers and authorities (this is our strength). And thus, by the conclusion of Paul's prayer, we see that the hope, the wealth, and the power that Paul is eager for the eyes of our hearts to see are all of a piece. We ought, as God's people, to be possessed of an unimaginable confidence.

Do you pray with that kind of confidence? Do you come to the throne of God in the hope, wealth, and power of God's Holy Spirit? In the firm knowledge of your resurrection from the dead? With your soul firmly planted in the saving and conquering work of Jesus Christ? In the confident assurance that you are Christ's body, the Church, and therefore the agent of God's redemptive work in the world? As we meditate on these characteristics of God's power—the hope, the wealth, and the strength—each should create profound confidence in our lives; we need not fear death; we possess the Spirit of the Holy God as an inheritance and present reality; and as the Church we sit on the Throne of God with Christ in power over all earthly and Heavenly authorities.

Having access to power like this—to a reason for confidence such as this—and neglecting to use it is like owning a winning lottery ticket that you never cash. And yet few people pray with this confidence. As believers we are possessed of unimaginable power that we rarely access. Why should this be? I've identified four reasons why we don't pray with confidence.

First, we do not pray with confidence in God's power because we are ignorant of the power that is available to us. I cannot think of a time when I've heard a sermon on why our hope for the resurrection of the dead should give us confidence in the present. Sure, we can have confidence when we die—but what about the resurrection power for today? How are we learning about our inheritance as God's beloved children now? And are we living our lives as if Jesus really was sitting and reigning on the throne of heaven, with us as his Church reigning with him? You cannot possibly pray in confidence when you are unaware of your reasons for confidence.

Second, we do not pray with confidence in God's power because when we pray we are trusting in our own power rather than God's. Our confidence is misplaced. We are not truly trusting in Christ the conquering and saving King. And so we trust in our own righteousness, in our own image, in certain prayer forms, and in a host of other things. We pray by our own power when we attempt to do prayer certain ways, with certain words, in certain times, and in certain places. At other times, we hope that our fervency or our self-punishment will somehow win us special access to God. Our prayers are powerless because in them we are seeking to use our power to leverage God to do our will, rather than submit to God's power so that we can learn His will.

Third, we do not pray with confidence in God's power because we lack faith. We doubt that God is good enough, or strong enough, or caring enough to act in our circumstances. And we do this because we spend too much time gazing at our circumstances and our world, and not enough time gazing at God. This is precisely the story of Peter walking on water with Jesus in Matthew 14. As long as Peter's eyes were on Christ, he was supported—he had firm footing and confidence in what by all appearances (and reality!) was an impossible situation. But as soon as Peter took his eyes from Christ and looked instead at the wind and waves—his circumstances—then he began to sink like the rock he was. So also us, because our confidence in God's power will naturally have strength in proportion to the amount of time we've spent gazing upon and taking in His power.

Fourth, we do not pray with confidence in God's power because we aren't praying at all; in the words of James, "You do not have because you do not ask God" (James 4:2 NIV). This is just another expression of unbelief and of pride (misplaced confidence). We live our lives attempting our own control, subsisting by our own meagre and feeble strength when the power of God is available to us.

CONFIDENCE IN GOD'S LOVE

While confidence in God's magnificent power provides the first "foot" of our confidence in prayer, the other foot, to continue the metaphor, is to trust in God's love. And, in the same way as with God's power, as we contemplate, understand, and apprehend the love of God in our lives, our posture before Him will also grow with remarkable confidence. Interestingly, this love of God is the subject of Paul's other great prayer from the letter of Ephesians, this time at the close of chapter 3. There Paul says the following:

Because of this, I bend my knee in prayer to the Father—from Whom all fatherhood in heaven and on earth is named—that He should give to you power from the wealth of His glory to strengthen, by means of His Spirit, your inner man; that Christ should dwell in your hearts through faith; that, having been rooted and established in love, you should be enabled to grasp with all the saints what is the breadth and length and height and depth [of His love], and to know, with superabundant knowledge, the love of Christ, in order that you may be filled to all the fullness of God. (Ephesians 3:14-19, author's translation)

Paul's elegant prayer has a beautiful progression to it—it moves upwards, and is not unlike the building of a living "house" of love. What is not immediately clear in English is that the first work that Paul requests for the Ephesian believers is in the middle of the prayer at verse 17. There, he asks that they be rooted and established in love. These are the foundations of the house. To have roots in love means that love is the water that we draw up through the roots of our lives, becoming the very sap of our existence. Paul thus prays that God's love would be our lifeblood, energizing and strengthening us at our most basic, inner levels. Along with this rootedness, he prays that we be established upon love; that love would be the foundation of our house as well, the firm and secure ground on which all else is built. Then comes the petition in verse 16, that God would give us power to be strengthened in our inner man. This strengthening, I believe, is like the walls of the house being firmed—except the house is our souls. Following this (or perhaps parallel to it), Christ dwells in our hearts by faith. Here the inner man, rooted in love, established upon love, and strengthened by God's power, is further strengthened with the presence of the Person of Love. The goal of this process is revealed in verses 18-19: that we might know—really know—the superabundant reaches of God's love —its heights, breadths and depths. Love, then, is beneath us, love surrounds us, love dwells within us, and love is the content of our knowledge. That knowledge adds new meaning to the psalmist's phrase that, "If I go up to the Heavens you are there; if I make my bed in Sheol, you are there" (Psalm 139:8 NIV). The love of God, in other words, is an inescapable reality in the universe. All this Paul prays so that we might be filled with the all the fullness of God; that the love of God would saturate and transform our lives, exalting us to the fullness of God Himself.

How do we learn, or apprehend, the love of God? The answer of the scriptures is that we learn love as we look at Jesus. John 3:16 is a verse with which people are so familiar that we have missed something important within it. Most of us have learned a version like this: "For God so loved the world that he gave his only begotten son, that whoever believes in him will not die but have eternal life." And I'm pretty sure that the average person reading that verse thinks, as I did for a long time, that that word "so" means "so much"—that God loved the world *so much* that He gave His son. But that word "so" is really the word for "in this way"—it describes not the *extent* but the *manner* of God's love. In other words—and this is the message of John's gospel as a whole—we know, we comprehend, we really get what God's love is by looking at Christ. Consequently we can paraphrase John 3:16 in the following way: "This is the manner of God's love for us: that He gave His son for us." The son is given so that the world can know the love of God. We learn love by looking at Jesus.

In what ways, then, is the love of God a warrant for confidence? Perhaps the most important way is that when we stand in the love and power of God we are forgiven. God, we just observed, has showed us His love by giving us His son, Jesus, and Jesus shows us the love of the Father by giving up his life on a Roman cross. "Greater love," Jesus says, "has no one than this: that he lay down his life for his friends" (John 15:13 NIV). Jesus' death and resurrection is the loving power of God on display for our salvation; the Son's life of love is the foundation of our salvation. And therefore, although we come to God as sinful people, broken and hurting, at the same time we stand before Him because of Christ's work as forgiven people. This further reveals why humility comes first in prayer, and love follows after; because humility creates the conditions for confession, and when we confess our sins God meets us with His abundant love. Our repentance is always greeted by the Father's loving embrace.

Extending from the effects of our forgiveness, when we stand confident in the love of God we do not have to earn God's approval. When Jesus is baptized and the Holy Spirit descends on him, the onlookers hear a voice from heaven that announces, "This is my son, whom I love; with him I am well pleased" (Matthew 3:17 NIV). One of the things that is re-markable about this divine statement is that Jesus hasn't done anything yet. No healings, no exorcisms, no teachings, nothing. God the Father offers Jesus, His beloved son, approval that is unconditional. Part of the good news of the Gospel of Christ is that when we become sons and daughters of God—God's special children—then we too become beneficiaries of the unconditional love of God. When we stand in God's love then we need do nothing to earn God's approval.

The love of God is also a warrant for our confidence because God's love is the power that abolishes our fear. In the words of John, "Perfect love casts out fear" (1 John 4:18). Where love reigns, fear is abolished, destroyed, and utterly robbed of its power. Where God's love rules, the need for self-justification is eliminated, the possibility of rejection is removed, forgiveness of sins is bestowed, and anxiety is crushed. And while our anxiety, revealing our need for God, may drive us to pray, we do not pray in anxiety. We do not pray in the fear that our requests may not be heard, or that we haven't prayed appropriately. The love of God makes such fears impossible. And hence Paul says in Philippians 4:6 (NIV), "Do not worry, but in everything by prayers and petitions with thanksgiving make known your requests to God." We are thankful and not anxious in prayer because the love of God goes before us and surrounds us.

The more we trust in God's love, the more of God's love we will experience. This is because it is only when we are willing to risk abandoning our pretension in humility that we discover the great depths of God's love for us. We are instructed to "Taste and see that the LORD is good"—to give Him a try; to risk it; to see what kind of God He really is (Psalm 34:8 NIV). And those first steps of self-humbling involve genuine risk on our part. After all, there is a great deal of personal risk in losing the fig leaves of our pretension—we spend our whole lives pretending to be other than we are, hoping that people will like us. And it is because of this that the shedding of our lifelong pretences can be painful and threatening. But this is again why humility is the first step, the foundational posture, to approaching God in prayer. As anyone who has loved knows, in disclosing yourself to another person—in allowing yourself to be loved for who you are—there is always a risk. If I reveal my true self, will I be accepted? If I undress (figuratively speaking) will I be mocked? Having spent our lives dressing up in order to hide, the real business of love can only begin when we undress—when we stop pretending to be people we aren't. In the same way, it is only when we have stripped ourselves of our pretences in prayer that we are finally in a position to grasp just how loving God really is toward us. Our first steps of trust are met eagerly by a God Who is eager to prove Himself trustworthy and loving. And in the perfect trust which is generated by the love of God toward us we find freedom to truly bare our deepest souls—to really and truly be ourselves in the presence of God.

Thus God's love is the ground on which we build, the sap from which we are nourished, the walls that secure us. His love is manifest to us in the presence of Christ dwelling in our hearts, which causes us to shoot upwards in understanding worship of that love. And this love, together with the power of God revealed in Christ, provides the firm foundation of our confidence in prayer. We stand firm in prayer on the twin feet of the power and love of God.

Here, then, is how we have learned to pray so far—not with particular words, but with particular postures. We begin by approaching God with a posture of humility, rejecting our pretence. We come to God as we are, seeking Him as He is, in a genuine conversation. And it is only then that we can address our misplaced confidence. This progression is appropriate, because we cannot truly address our false confidence until we have stripped away our pretence; there is always an initial step of humility that is necessary to apprehend God's love, like a clearing of the rubble before a real work can begin. After all, people who pretend that they are all right cannot receive God's forgiving love any more than a person who pretends he is healthy can benefit from a doctor. In other words, recognizing our need for God's love is a prerequisite to apprehending it. This, by the way, is the meaning of the "unforgivable sin"—it is unforgivable not because it is of a degree worse than other sins, but because it is itself the rejection of forgiveness. As a terminally sick person who rejects the help of an able physician will die of his illness, so a person who rejects his need for God cannot receive God's forgiveness.[*]

With humility in place, we then stand with a posture of confidence that is established upon the twin foundations of God's power and God's love. These are the unshakable foundations of the Christian faith, and our posture of confidence in prayer will be proportionate to our reflection upon, apprehension of, and belief in these foundations. Thus, our certain knowledge of God's unshakable power and love will undergird all our prayers. It is at this point that something unique happens. In the same way that misplaced confidence generates a false edifice (that is, pretence), proper confidence (a right

---

[*] Mark 3:20-30. The metaphor of the physician is an appropriate parallel to Jesus' teaching. In Jesus' story he implies that he is the one who has bound the strong man, Satan. And the looming question for the Pharisees is that if they reject Jesus—who has power to defeat Satan—who will remain to help them? In rejecting Christ they have rejected the only one with power to save them—they have tied the hands of the physician and are unforgivable because they have rejected the very source of forgiveness.

foundation) begs an edifice of its own. Where trusting in a lie creates false personalities, trusting in what is true should produce genuine personalities. And so, when we stand as we are before God, and upon His foundations, the humble confidence that is produced will demand a holy and different attitude to accompany it. This attitude is the third posture of prayer: boldness.

BOLDNESS

If we are a people whose trust is anchored on the absolute power of God, whose identities cannot be threatened because they are surrounded and enriched by the love of God, then our lives ought to display the exhilarating thrill of genuine confidence in God. We ought to be a fearless and bold people; impervious, unassailable, endowed with a humble confidence that shatters the pretence of the prideful and gives birth to hope in the struggling. The humble boldness of Christians ought to be shocking to the pretence of the world, our power in Christ stunning, our freedom because of the all-encompassing love of God desirable. To put it simply, if the God of the Bible really is our God, if we really believe our own theology, then we ought to be a *very* bold people.

If the first two postures are preparatory to prayer—almost like learning to stand—then in boldness we take our first steps toward God. With lives that are rooted in proper confidence we can pray, walking forward in faith with a posture of boldness.

Humility grows when we contemplate God's holiness, confidence when we contemplate His power and love, and boldness blossoms when we contemplate the Fatherhood of God. In boldness, we have direct access to God the Father through the Son. We do not fear to enter directly into the holy of holies and approach His throne with requests. Because of the work of Christ the veil of the temple has been torn, and thus we need no intermediaries—no priests or pastors, no saints or holy days, no church buildings or sacred sites are needed to pray. Every believer in Christ has as his and her inherited right the privilege of direct access to God in prayer.

In boldness we pray to God as our Father. And not only as Father but as our Abba Father—one dear to us, one on whose knee we feel free to run up and sit. With God as our Abba we need never fear to request any good thing from Him. After all, Jesus teaches us in Matthew 7:11 that if we, who are wicked, know how to give good gifts to our children, won't God do so much more for us? If your son asks for bread, will you give him a stone? If he asks for a fish, do you deceive him with a snake? God knows our needs and loves His children—He will provide. What is more, as beloved children we never need to beg from our Father. We do not come to God as paupers asking for crusts of bread, or as homeless vagabonds asking for spare change. We come to God as beloved children. And therefore we never need fear to ask God for any good thing that we desire.

It is for the molding of these desires that Jesus has given us the Lord's Prayer, a prayer specifically crafted to shape our fundamental perceptions of reality. It is a prayer for the people of the Kingdom of God, and when we pray this prayer it brings our hearts into alignment with God's Reign. It is also, we should not be surprised to see, a very bold prayer. Consider that prayer again now:

Our Father in Heaven,
Let your Name be made holy,
Let your Kingdom come,
Let your will be done,
On earth may things be as they are in heaven.
Give to us today our bread for today,
And forgive us our sins, as we have forgiven those who sin against us,
And lead us not into temptation,
But deliver us from the Evil One.

There is a clear division in this prayer between the first five clauses and the closing four: the opening clauses align our hearts with God's mission in the world, shaping our desires. The closing ones ask God to equip us for that mission, meeting our needs.

The shaping of our desires begins with the first words of the prayer: we address ourselves to "Our Father in Heaven." Here we speak to Who God is (our heavenly Father) in light of who we are (His beloved children). We turn our hearts toward a loving, powerful Father who is eager to hear our requests. After this address we begin to pray in petitions. First, we ask Him to, "Let Your Name be made holy." The Name of God is a representation of and testimony to His character and mighty deeds; it is shorthand for God's fame on earth. So when we petition God to make His own Name holy, we are asking God to make the knowledge of Himself great among all people, to reveal Himself in mighty deeds, to show His sanctifying power in the Church, and to convict the world of sin. This petition dramatically shapes our own desires when we recognize that, in this world, we are the people who either tarnish or sanctify God's Name. "Make Your Name holy" is, because we are Gods' representatives on earth, in some senses synonymous with "Make *us* holy." Following this we pray, "Let Your Kingdom come." We acknowledge that although God reigns from on high with Christ, His Kingdom is not complete in our world; there is a gap between heaven and earth which we are asking God to close. After this we ask God to, "Let Your will be done." Echoing Jesus' great prayer in the Garden of Gethsemane (Luke 22:42), that "Not my will but Yours be done," we pray each day for the will of God, and not our will, to be performed in our lives. With this petition we recognize that it is only in the perfect subjection of our will to God's will—from within the submission of our power and control to His hands and care—that we may ask for anything in His name and expect to receive it in faith. After all, it is the business of God to make His Name holy and to advance His Kingdom in the world; when we make ourselves willing vessels of that great work then God does His works through us. His Name and His Kingdom advance through our submissive and willing lives. The ultimate goal of these requests—and indeed of all human reality—is summarized in the bridging line between God's Kingdom and our needs, "As things are in heaven may they be on earth." In other words, we are asking for harmony, for *shalom*, for the ultimate reconciliation between heaven and earth.

From the exalted work of God's Kingdom mission, which reorients our minds and hearts in prayer, we turn again to God the loving and caring Father. And in the concluding half of the prayer we ask for those things we require to be able to fulfill our part of God's Kingdom mission in the world. We ask God to meet our needs. We need bread, God, so that our bodies survive. We need forgiveness, God, so that we can stand in your presence. We must forgive others, God, so that we don't hold Your forgiveness in contempt. And we need protection, Lord God, both from the temptations which are common to our species and from the Evil One who delights in our destruction.

From within this matrix of requests we discover the utter and remarkable freedom of prayer: that when we live within the will of Almighty God, passionate about His mission in the world to advance His Name and Kingdom through us and our lives, then we may freely ask whatever we like, boldly, in the name of the Father, and He will answer us. It is from within this posture of prayer, I believe, that Jesus' words to his disciples are fulfilled, that "whatever you ask, believe that you will receive, and it will be done for you" (Mark 11:24, author's translation). Because when we stand humbly, confident, and boldly—when we stand as we really are and talk to God as He really is—then we will never ask Him for something which violates His will. We won't be able to.

PUTTING IT TO PRACTICE

In this chapter I have written about deep, habitual practices of the Christian heart in prayer. It should be clear, if it is not already, that humility, confidence, and boldness are lifelong habits and not momentary impulses. Because of this, we cannot wait to be perfectly humble, confident, and bold to pray—if we did we would never start! And so it remains to speak to two final questions about how to pray. First, how do I begin to pray in private? And second, how do I pray in public? In both cases, the answer is similar: need is the fountain of prayer, and in all your prayers—whether public or private—the beginning step is to admit your neediness before God and then speak to Him as you are, out of that neediness. Use your own words. Speak with your own voice. Speak to God what is on your heart. If you find that you need some structure to organize your thoughts, you can use the Lord's Prayer to guide you, or even a prayer acronym such as A.C.T.S. (Adoration, Confession, Thanksgiving, Supplication). You could even use a simple set of prayers like the following ones to get you on the right track:

Dear God, you are God and I am not (Humility).

You are able (Confidence in his power).

You love us (Confidence in his love).

In boldness we ask... (Fill in your requests)

But again, there are no right words for prayer, and these are only guides—perhaps even crutches—to get you started. If you are praying in public, try to forget the room of people around you; forget that anyone is listening but God, and speak to Him and Him alone. In either situation, whether praying publicly or privately, the principles of prayer are the same. Hence, whether you are alone or in front of a thousand people, prayer is a simple matter of speaking your (or your community's) needs to God. Remember, then, as you speak, that you are in the presence of an All-Powerful God—that any and every circumstance of your life is within His power to control and change.

Remember as well that you are in the presence of an All-Loving God—one Who has given the life of His son for your life, Who embraces you and calls you His beloved child. Thus, the origin and generation of all our prayers is our neediness, and the more authentically needy you are, and the more you grow to depend upon the perfect power and love of God, the more bold you will become—in faith, in life, and especially in prayer.

There is no place, in true Christian prayer, for fearful and timid posturing. There is no room for the tired antics of fig-leaf and finger-pointing prayers. There are no special words or special times or special places. Instead, we approach God at any time with right posture: humbly, recognizing God's holiness; confidently, acknowledging His power and love; and with the boldness of beloved children. With these postures in place, you may ask whatever you like.

Questions for Group Discussion

Which of the postures of prayer—humility, confidence in God's power, confidence in God's love, and boldness—is easiest for you? Which is most difficult?

What are some ways that you, personally, can work to build these postures into your life with God?

Exercise: Pray through the Lord's Prayer and expand upon each clause—Pray, "Our Father, who is in heaven," then speak more about Who He is and what He does. Then pray, "Make Your Name Holy," and expand on what that would look like. Continue throughout the prayer, expanding each clause accordingly.

IV
ANSWERS TO PRAYER, PART 1
Hearing God's Voice

Once, while walking among the houses where I grew up, I came upon one of my fellow neighborhood kids, crying in a tree. He was in distress, I found out, because he had just lost a baseball game. But the game wasn't his main problem; the real problem was that he and two friends had followed Jesus' instruction in Matthew 18—that whenever two or three are gathered in his name, whatever they ask he would do for them (Matt 18:19-20). Three of them had gotten together and asked to win the game, and yet they had lost. They had followed Jesus' instructions, and Jesus had, apparently, let them down. What went wrong?

Looking back, there is a clear theological problem with his prayer, and it is such a common error that I must take a moment to address it. Jesus, when he speaks these words in Matthew 18, is not instructing us on how to maximize our prayer impact—as if we could, by assembling two or three people together, somehow *leverage* God to do our will, or as if the magic number "two or three" makes it so that God can't say no. This becomes clear when we realize that Jesus does not pull the number "two or three" out of thin air, but is invoking a command from the book of Deuteronomy that "a matter must be established by the testimony of two or three witnesses" (Deut 19:15 NIV). What that means is that Jesus is, in no way whatsoever, describing a kind of spiritual "quorum" for petitionary prayer. Rather, he is instructing his followers in procedure for administrating Church discipline (which is, broadly, the subject of Matthew 18). In short, Matthew 18 isn't about petitionary prayer, or even how many people need to be present for Jesus to manifest himself, but rather excommunication. It is, then, not a very good scripture with which to begin a church prayer meeting.

Returning, however, to my childhood friend's experience of unanswered prayer—and regardless of the particular error that motivated that prayer—his experience brings into crucial focus a question that each of us faces: why doesn't God answer all of our prayers? Is He even listening?

Dealing with answers may actually be the riskiest part of petitionary prayer. After all, everything I've said so far about prayer presumes that God does, in fact, *answer* prayers; that He responds to our requests; that it is not in any way unreasonable to expect Him to do things in our lives in response to the petitions we make in prayer. The idea of prayer to a caring, sovereign, and divine being presupposes that we are not engaging merely in wishful thinking or "positive thoughts." Furthermore, if we adopt the postures of which I have spoken —approaching God as we are, secure in His power, embraced by His love, and bold in our requests—then a byproduct of all these should be an unavoidable sense of expectation. When we pray we ought to pray with hope. What all this adds up to is that if God does answer prayer, then all is well and good. But if He doesn't, then what does that say about Him? Doesn't the entire concept of petitionary prayer become a kind of test for God's goodness, if not His very existence?

Seeking answers in petitionary prayer is not risky to God alone, but to us as well. When we make a sincere request to God we are risking something of ourselves in the process—all requests cost something to the asker. The act of laying down our power, of relinquishing our pretence and embracing the self-humbling of really *asking* God to do something in our lives costs us something. We risk a sacred and valuable part of our souls when we make requests of God. As we ponder these risks an ominous question may begin to take form in the dark recesses of our minds: "What if I do all that I need to pray in petitions but God says nothing?"

What makes this worse is the sober admission that "hearing God speak" is by no means a guaranteed, or even seemingly common, experience for people. Most people seem to go through life not hearing God at all. Even worse, the people who *do* claim to hear God are often unreliable sources, better suited, perhaps, for the asylum than the pulpit. And as a consequence of all this, prayer is again reduced to a kind of pipe dream, a fancy of wishful thinkers. Like children writing letters to Santa Claus, the faithful carefully address their prayers to the North Pole, but we all know (*wink wink*) there's nothing really there. Prayer is nice in the way that positive thinking is nice; you might feel better after doing it, but you certainly shouldn't expect anything from it—and heaven forbid you place any *hope* on it!

In stark contrast to this, the Bible is a lengthy record of God speaking to His people and acting in their lives—and while He speaks directly to some people and indirectly to others, throughout the Bible God is always documented as having something to say. The psalmist goes so far as to present the created order itself as a voice of God speaking constantly to us, proclaiming that "The heavens declare the glory of God... Day after day they pour forth speech" (Psalm 19:1-2 NIV). In the book of Romans Paul points to the created world as evidence of God's existence, providing testimony against the wicked who are, as a consequence, without excuse (Romans 1:19-20). In John's Gospel, of course, Jesus himself is described as the Word of God—God, speaking to us through the life and flesh of Jesus. The Bible is a record throughout of a speaking, talkative God, and when we pray in petitions we are praying to this highly verbose God. Our prayers are directed toward a God who answers prayers, and therefore with the Psalmist again we pray, "In the morning, O LORD, you hear my voice; in the morning I lay my requests before you and wait *in expectation*" (Psalm 5:3 NIV, emphasis mine). The act of prayer presupposes that God both hears and answers our requests. Hope and expectation in petitionary prayer is not a pipe dream, but a mandate.

This, then, is the scope of our dilemma: on the one hand the Bible documents a talkative God, while on the other hand human experience testifies (seemingly) to God's ominous silence in a lengthy record of unanswered prayers. This dilemma ought to alarm us. If prayer really is as foundational to the Christian life as I have suggested, then dealing with God's silence is as important a task as understanding His answers.

Notably, the Bible itself is not silent on the subject of God's silence, and the book of Job is a sustained examination of the silence of God—particularly in the face of tragedy. Job, in that story, loses his children, his wealth, and his health in tragic short succession because of what amounts to a bet between God and Satan. Destitute, he is left with a nagging wife and three friends who are full of noisome advice. Their words, far from alleviating or comforting Job in his pain, instead magnify God's looming silence and increase Job's suffering. The majority of the book as it unfolds documents not God explaining Himself to Job, but Job and his three friends trying to manage and explain the silence of God. When God does speak at the end of the book, His words are not so much an answer to Job's questions as they are an experience. God's thundering announcements from the whirlwind fill the silence, not with answers, but with declarations: "I am real. I control the universe. Now stop questioning my judgment. You don't understand these things." The book of Job refuses to minimize human grief with simple answers.

Job's story casts a stark and revealing light on all our experiences of God's silence. And it does this primarily because there is no place in human experience where the silence of God looms larger—no place where our doubt is more poignant—than when we experience tragedy. Consider for a moment the prayer, "Why, God?" which has become something of a cinematic joke in our culture. Close up, we hear and see a lonely man shouting these words bitterly to the heavens. While they reverberate through the air, the camera swoops upwards revealing him standing utterly alone in his grief. All melodrama aside, the scenario points to something common in human life. Watch the news and you will see regular people standing in the rubble of their homes after tornadoes, hurricanes and earthquakes, asking "Why?" You will see average people like you and me who have lost everything because of circumstances out of their control—a bank fails, a fire consumes their property—and they, too, ask "Why?" Turn to your own lives and you will find an equal number of scenarios; mothers who have lost children, husbands who have lost wives, parents whose children are handicapped, all of them asking "Why?" You yourself have experienced pain and tragedy in your life and asked, "Why?" The Person, of course, from Whom we are all seeking an answer is God Himself. And yet very rarely in the movie, and without much greater frequency in our lives, does anyone seem to receive an answer to this prayer. God's apparent silence looms largest in our moments of tragedy.

Why does tragedy magnify silence? It does this because need occasions prayer in our lives, and the greater the need, the greater the volume of our prayers. When tragedy comes into our lives (and it comes to all our lives) our levels of need are at their highest. Like Job we are stretched—physically, emotionally, psychologically—to the very limits of our personalities, and in our severe need we pray with all our might. Consequently, inasmuch as need always awakens our senses (remember how the need to find a lost object causes us to look everywhere), so tragedy sets our senses afire. Hence, the silence feels oppressively greater at these times for the simple reason that in the moments of tragedy we strain our ears to hear God more than in our regular lives. We strain so intensely for a particular sound that its absence feels all the more cavernous— like waiting for a phone that never rings, or a bus that isn't coming. And in point of fact, God's silence is so great in those moments that all attempts to explain God's actions, whether by exoneration or blame, succeed only in magnifying the silence itself. And that is why the many words of gospel ministers and well-intentioned believers, who seem desperate to explain, or justify, or make sense of God's awful silence in those moments, is revealed for the thin and tired excuse-mongering that it is. Job's friends are poor counsel and even worse support in the midst of his suffering.

And yet God is not silent. He answers prayer all the time. He is constantly speaking to you and me as thunderously as He did to Job, and the testimony of the Bible to a talkative God is as true today as it was in the ancient world. How, then, do we resolve the dilemma between the speaking and silent ex-periences of God? The answer may be hard to hear, because in the end, the problem is not that God isn't speaking, but that we are deaf to His voice. And this, in fact, is God's own witness against us as recorded in the scriptures. In Deuteronomy, the Psalms, Isaiah, Jeremiah, Ezekiel, and then in the words of Jesus himself, we are pronounced to be a people who have ears but do not hear, and eyes but do not see.[*] The consistent diagnosis of scripture is that we are spiritually deaf and blind to the manifold sounding of the voice of God.

---

[*] See, for example, Deuteronomy 29:3-5, Psalm 115, Isaiah 6:10, Jeremiah 5:21, Ezekiel 12:2, Mark 4:12 (quoting Isaiah), and other places as well.

THE FIRST DEAFNESS

I believe that we humans are deaf to God's voice—we don't hear answers to our prayers—for three reasons. And the first reason that we don't hear answers is because we weren't praying to God in the first place. Prayer, in tragedy, is instinctual; the great need that tragedy places upon us causes us to call out to a divine being greater than we are. But the instinct of prayer does not imply that the object of prayer will be correct. All people pray, but relatively few know to whom they are praying. They do not know who He is; they do not know the kinds of things He does. And rather than asking a personal and divinely revealed God to act on their behalf, they are submitting petitions to an unknown, but hopefully benign, cosmic force. Because they are essentially praying to someone who isn't there, these prayers are no more effective than prayers to Santa Claus or the Easter Bunny. Many of the people who bemoan the silence of God in prayer are like a person who complains that the television show he wants to watch is not on, while all along the real problem is that he has tuned in to the wrong channel. The problem is not the show, the problem is you. And hence many do not hear God when they pray because they have not been praying to God.*

---

* Allow me to clarify, briefly, that in some sense we are *always* praying to a God we don't know because nobody can ever claim to know God *fully* (which is an impossibility). In fact, when we first come to faith in God we pray to a God we know only marginally *if at all*. I am in no way, therefore, advocating that we must have a perfect knowledge of God before we can hear His voice. However, we must acknowledge that our incapacity to know God fully does not mean we can abdicate our need to seek Him continually; and that if you are seeking answers to your prayers, then you must also be seeking His particular voice.

A compounded effect of these essentially misguided prayers is that, when God does speak, these people don't know the sound of His voice. Because they have never learned Who He is, they are ignorant of Him when He speaks. This, I fear, is a problem far more pervasive than we might suspect, because there are a host of people who profess faith in God who have never taken the time to learn about Him through, primarily, the reading of the scriptures. In the place of God, they have turned to other voices in their lives for guidance—horoscopes, talk shows, friends. They are listening, intently, for the voice of God in all the wrong places. Such people channel surf through all the options of spirituality, all the while neglecting the one true option they crave to hear. In their confusion they have muddled their ability to hear God speak; their ears filled with all the wrong channels, they are ignorant of God's authentic voice. As a consequence of these things the vast majority of people who pray—even Christians who pray—are praying to a Being that they don't know, Whose word they have never read, Whose character they are unfamiliar with, Whose ways of acting in the world they do not know. In short, many people who pray are like pilgrims to the Aeropagus who offer petitions to unknown gods, just in case (Acts 17:23). Once again, they do not get answers to their prayers because they don't know the God they are praying to.

If you want to hear God's voice in your life, then you must, you absolutely must, you unavoidably must, *learn* what His voice sounds like. You must learn what kind of God He is, how He acts, what kinds of things He does in the world. And I will even go so far as to say that you have no right to claim that God is silent in your life if you are not reading His book on a regular basis. Because it is only a growing sense of the character and consistency of the Lord God that will counteract this deafness and open our ears to hear His voice give us answers in prayer. And we discover who God is, primarily, when we read the scriptures.

In the scriptures we learn that "I the LORD do not change" (Malachi 3:6 NIV). We change, of course. We are inconstant and fickle; but God is perfect in His commitment to us. And how we see Him behave and act in the past is guaranteed to be in accordance with how He will act both in our present lives and in the future as well. Therefore we come to know God's character by studying the record of His actions in the past. This, of course, is a principle that is true for all people, because character is revealed in action. If I claim that I am good, that in itself is meaningless—it is only when I do things that are good that you can validate the truth or falsehood of my statement. In this way, the scriptures, by documenting the actions of God, testify to God's eternal and unchanging character. We get to know God by seeing how He works, and when we see how He worked in the past we will be equipped to look for Him in our everyday lives.

What is the character of God as revealed in the scriptures? When we speak of His character we employ words—ideas, really—like Justice, Mercy, Grace, Love, Power, and Peace (i.e., *shalom*). We say that God is each of these things, and yet so much more than even the sum of them. We say that He is absolutely Holy, and completely Good. We observe how He hates wickedness and loves righteousness. We discern that He is the source of life and the arbiter of death. He controls all things. And the purest, most illuminating focal point for the character of God is the study of the life of Jesus; we get to see what God looks like best and hear what He sounds like most clearly when we fix our eyes upon Jesus Christ. And hence the author of Hebrews can affirm, echoing Malachi, that "Jesus Christ is the same yesterday and today and forever" (Hebrews 13:8 NIV). He is constant and trustworthy in all things.

Because God's character is unchanging in this way, He will never say anything to anyone that contradicts His word in the scriptures. The voice of God in your life will always be in conformity with His word in the Bible. This, in part, is the essence of what it means for the Bible to be called a *canon*. The word canon means measuring rod, and used of the Christian Bible it signifies that these books are the standard against which our lives and doctrines must be measured. If you have no sense of measurement, how can you judge whether a thing is right or not? If you have no sense of direction, how can you get anywhere in life? The study of the scriptures—the canon— provides us with these fundamental standards which allow us to recognize and obey the voice of God.

THE SECOND DEAFNESS

The second reason why we don't hear God's voice—why we don't get answers in prayer—is because we aren't actually listening for Him. We speak to God, offering a litany of prayers, but never take the time to attend to His responses. In this we are like people who talk all the time but never listen— people with whom you can never get in a word edgewise because they are so busy listening to the sound of their own voices. Except that in our cases it is God who can't slip in the edgewise word. In a real way, then, we are deaf because we have plugged our ears from hearing God's voice in our lives.

At times, we are deaf because we are disobedient; we have plugged our ears because we don't like what God is saying to us. In these circumstances God has spoken to us clearly—in His scriptures or by placing a burden on our hearts—and we have refused to do what He asked. And in flat-out refusing the voice of God, God's voice becomes silent. We turn to God in frustration and say, "Why aren't you speaking to me?" And God says in response, "I did speak to you; you just didn't listen." Much of the time, the call to obedience is in relation to some sin in our hearts. God has asked you to deal with an area of sin, and you are resisting Him. As long as we choose the sin rather than God, God will be largely silent toward us.

But often we are deaf out of neglect. Here we plug our ears from hearing God's voice when we allow the noise of life to crowd and interfere with God's voice. It is as if we have gone to a loud restaurant to meet with God. But rather than attending to God and His answers, we talk on our phones, or check our emails, or listen to the people around us, or watch the television in the corner above His head. We ask God for things in prayer, but aren't paying attention when He answers. And the truth of the matter is that in no meaningful relationship in your life would you hold an important conversation at a noisy bar—music blaring and a large crowd of boisterous revelers at hand. Instead, you will go somewhere quiet where you can really hear each other. But when it comes to God, we refuse to create this space. And this, in part, is because we live in a world that is terrified of silence. As nature abhors a vacuum, so our world abhors silent reflection.

Because of this, if we are not careful, the cacophonous sounds of our world will always crowd out the voice of God. Everything calls for our attention: your phone, email, text messages, social media; your music is constant, television is always on, you are surfing the net at all hours; you are listening to the radio or watching YouTube; you are always with your friends and never alone. And it isn't just outward noise, because things like our work and general busyness are also anesthetics against the danger of silence. In a real way, by filling our lives with noise, we have medicated ourselves against the terror of silence. Truly, silence can be terrifying. If we are silent we will be forced to take stock of our lives—we might have to engage in some self-reflection. And when we do this we may not like what we see. Noise, therefore, helps us cope with the threat of silent reflection, and we avoid silence like a self-conscious person avoids a mirror—if we never stop to look perhaps we can forget what we don't like about ourselves. But the fear of self-reflection is not our only fear; sometimes, if we're honest, we admit that we fill our lives with noise so that we *won't* have to hear God speak to us. We know what He's going to say and we're afraid. God is speaking, but we've got our eyes shut tight and our fingers in our ears.

Our self-medication through noise, the noise we use as an antidote to our anxiety, dulls us to God's voice—the one true voice we really need to hear—and blocks us from receiving the peace that can only be achieved when we have first embraced silence. Against our culture of noise Jesus pronounces in the Second Beatitude that "Blessed are they who mourn, for they shall be comforted" (Matt 5:4). And I take this to mean that Jesus is not speaking merely to those who are sad, but rather that comfort is the reward given to those who are willing to mourn, people who have consciously rejected all the self-soothing of our world. And the principle is this: as long as we embrace escape from the pain of the world through medication, we cannot possess real healing; as long as we deceive ourselves into thinking that everything is right in the world, we cannot experience God's transformation; as long as medicating noise dominates our inner lives, we cannot hear the voice of God. Therefore, against the logic that medicating our silences will stem the pain of our lives, Jesus teaches us that only the people who are willing to mourn can be comforted—truly comforted, consoled, and brought peace. Because true peace comes from God alone, and not from any of the earthly things to which we turn for satisfaction.

Silence is scary, but it is indispensable if we would hear God's voice. Therefore we must have planned and regular times of silence where we filter out the conflicting voices and focus on God's voice alone. Silence such as this will take time. It cannot be achieved "on the fly," but requires that we create an environment in which to experience it. Silence is also difficult. It is something most of us have spent our lives avoiding, and the first endeavors into real silence may be terrifying. What people fear in silence, perhaps rightly, is that when we begin to close the valve on the noise of our lives the inner noise of our hearts and minds begins to well up. Things you didn't plan to think about suddenly loom large in your mind. Things you don't want to think about at all suddenly nag and nettle you. Anxieties, fears, tasks, sins—a host of inner voices are likely to crowd loudly in on us and need filtering. These distractions prove that the real target of silence in our ordinary lives is to quiet not the outer noise so much as to still our hearts before God.

How do we learn this silence? It will take, first, a time of real silence. Turn off everything you can around you. Walk away from your computer, television, radio, and phone. Find a place that is quiet. Crawl physically into your closet if necessary and close the door. Go to a park or on a walk outside away from people and distractions. Now, what will happen next is that thoughts and distractions will begin to swarm your mind. We have so learned the habit of noise that our souls do everything possible to fill our inner life with more noise. If you have ever stood in a doorframe and pressed your arms outward on the sides of the frame (for, say, about thirty seconds), you know that when you step out of the frame your arms will "float." The muscle memory of pressing outwards makes your arms perform this feat, and in the same way the memory of noise makes our minds fill with imagined noise. You have three options in responding to this noise. The first thing you can do, and this is instinctual, will be to attempt to bat these dist-ractions away like flies. My own experience is that this only leads to frustration; thoughts multiply faster than I can combat them. Second, you can think of one thing, focusing on that thing so that the other distractions begin to fade. You can focus on Christ, repeating his name over and over again. You could also repeat a simple Bible verse over and over in your mind (or out loud), such as "God is Love." As our attention upon God increases, the power of distractions decreases.* The third thing

---

* This is similar to a process that is sometimes called "Centering Prayer." If you would like more information regarding it, I recommend M. Basil Pennington's book of the same name (New York: Image Books, 2001).

you can do, and I think this is the most effective option, is to take hold of every thought and worry that comes into your mind and make a conscious decision to submit it to Christ. Don't debate it, don't argue with it, don't think about it, just submit it. It doesn't matter how important or irrelevant it seems to you in the moment—whether it's "What am I going to eat for lunch?" or "What career choice am I going to make?" Take the thought, and offer it to God in prayer—take every thought captive, as it were. In time, and less time than you might expect, I think you will find your heart and mind in a state of peace and rest. This process can also be helped along by means of a simple physical exercise, called "Hands down, hands up." Place your hands on your lap before you with the palms down. Offer each of the worries and concerns you have to God in a conscious act of submission. When you are done, turn your palms upward. The gesture, however subtle and small, is effective in readying our hearts to hear God's voice.[*]

When you've gone through a process such as this—an inner silencing of your heart and an awakening of your attention to God's voice—then you will have undergone a profound change in your heart and mind. Then you will know and recognize that real Christian silence is always a matter more of the heart than it is a physical reality. You can still your heart in this way in a crowd, on a bus, or at work. And although it will take a dedicated time of physical, emotional, and spiritual

---

[*] Sometimes, I employ the use of a small notepad, and if the fear of forgetfulness is too strong I will jot down thoughts and ideas as they come to me, postponing them until later. After all, sometimes God speaks to me in those thoughts and it's an important matter for me to remember them! The key, however, is that I use the notepad as a tool of submission—once the idea or thought is written down, I am no longer allowed to think about it.

silence to learn the sound of God's voice, and although this inner silence will need restoration from time to time with real retreat from the busyness of life, it remains a thing you can take within you to every aspect of your otherwise noisy life.

A story from the life of Elijah (1 Kings 19) gives shape to the dynamic between noise and silence. Elijah became distracted by his fears and anxieties; he allowed the concerns of his life to cloud his hearing of the voice of God, and in response Elijah became frustrated with God. God's response to Elijah is illuminating. First, God commanded Elijah to eat, drink, and sleep. In other words, Elijah required a period of rest and silence in his life. Then, God led Elijah to Mount Sinai where God caused a series of phenomena to appear before Elijah— there was a mighty wind, an earthquake, and a fire—but God was not in any of those things. Finally, there was a still, small voice—a whisper, really—and Elijah, we read, covered his face before the presence of God. We, like Elijah, get distracted by the worries of our world; we get focused on the outer noises so much that we miss the gentle and constant whisper of God in our everyday lives. And it is only when we have thus tuned out the multitudinous voices which clamor for our attention that we will finally be in a position to truly hear God speak. If we are not looking for God in the right place, we will miss His voice when He speaks.

THE THIRD DEAFNESS

The third and final reason why we don't hear God's voice—why we don't get answers in prayer—is because our requests are idolatrous. This is a difficult word to speak. It will be an even harder word to hear. But it is here where our attention to moments of human tragedy will offer us the clearest picture into the silence of God. This is because, like a magnifying glass for human experience, under the influence of tragedy we are enabled to perceive clearly some things that are perennially true but often obscured. Tragedy turns up the volume of our lives and enables us to "hear" why we are unable to hear answers to prayer as we should. In this, our thorough-going, pervasive idolatry is brought into sharp relief.

Human need instigates and occasions petitionary prayer, but our need during tragedy runs deeper than the common needs and anxieties of our ordinary lives. Hunger occasions merely a need for food, and loneliness indicates a need for companionship, but tragedy occasions awareness of our greatest human needs—things like meaning and significance. This is because in tragedy our most cherished securities—all the things we take for granted—are challenged and, at times, destroyed. An ordinary need is not having enough money for a different car; a tragedy is losing all your money when the bank fails. A need is asking God to allow your family to grow through childbirth; a tragedy is losing all your children to a disease. A need is asking God to heal you from a cold; tragedy is becoming a paraplegic in a car accident. The loss in tragedy always strikes at the subtle and deep foundations of our identities.

Tragedy unmakes us—everything in which we would normally have trusted is removed from us and we are left naked and helpless in life. The result is that nowhere do we pray more often or more intensely than when tragedy strikes. And it is this very unmaking that causes every human to pray during tragedy, even to a Being we don't know. This is because, shaken thus to our foundations, rendered utterly helpless in this world, we instinctively turn to the only remaining Being we believe can help us—the One outside our world. It is precisely *because* we have been robbed of our trust in anything else that we seek God in ways that normally we would not. Hence tragedy forces us to ask the deepest questions of significance in our lives: "Why am I here?" "What's the meaning of my life?" It is in those moments that we ask, "Why, God?"

But why should God seem so silent in these moments of great loss? The answer is sobering: humans are beings made for security—but we are made to be secure on one foundation only, that of God Himself. By taking our confidence and placing it on ourselves rather than God, as the story of the Fall of Mankind indicates, all our human priorities have been shifted into improper positions. As a consequence we draw our senses of identity and worth from our things, rather than God Who is the source of our things. Our identity is founded in our wealth, in our families, in our health, at times in our nations. Tragedy always strikes at these foundations—these false foundations—and the consequence is that we, who have depended on these false securities as anchors for our personalities and identities, are left profoundly adrift when they are removed from us.

Another way to talk about this false confidence is to employ the language of idolatry, and this is precisely what the Bible does. We must come to see that idolatry is not merely the craft, purchase, and worship of statues. It is far deeper and subtler than that. Idolatry is any place in your life where you are trusting in something *other* than God alone. Idolatry is a place in your life where you have power over something that you are withholding from God's control. It is a place in your heart which you have refused to submit to God, and to which you are clutching out of a desire for a kind of security. And all idolatry is poison to our spiritual lives. Still, it is the dominant image of the physical idol that gives rise to the Bible's frequent claim that "having eyes they do not see and ears they do not hear." These words allude to the muteness and deafness of stone and wood idols—a muteness and deafness that is promised to all who trust in such idols. In the end, this means that our experience of God's silence is not a matter of God not speaking; it is a matter of our hearts being hard to His voice. We do not hear God because we are idolatrous.

Under the influence of tragedy we search desperately for meaning, praying prayers to God that expose our desperate grasping for significance. But here is where the depth of our idolatry is truly exposed, because in our very petitions we betray our habit of drawing the significance of our lives from the stuff of our lives—from our idols. The requests we make are for God to restore us to the way things were "before"—to our spiritual complacency and laziness. Often the prayer "Why, God?" is really the prayer, "Why didn't you leave me alone?" The prayers in tragedy are usually, "Give me back my stuff" or "Don't take that away!" In short, our prayers during tragedy are requests for God to restore to us the idols of our lives, to give us the very things that poison our souls and keep us from experiencing God. Is it still a mystery why God should seem so silent during tragedy?

The experience of tragedy brightly illuminates something that is subtly and treacherously true of our everyday prayers: most of our requests are idolatrous. They are idolatrous when we pray to an idea of god that isn't really God—a god of convenience who does what we want, behaves like we do, and looks a great deal like us. We are idolaters when we pray to God as we want Him to be, rather than God as He is. We are idolaters when our requests violate His character and will, when we demand things from Him that offend His holiness. The majority of our prayers are idolatrous because in them we have made idols of our needs. We believe that what I need right now, in my opinion, is more important than what God says that I need. And as long as I clutch to my perception of how reality ought to work out for me, rather than allowing God to inform my reality, my prayers themselves will be for idols.

The first step to approaching God in genuine prayer is an attitude of humility—the real I speaking to the real God. In humility we strike at the pretence that is built upon our false confidence and come to God as real people. And yet the pretence of security that we find in our idols is the very apex of human false confidence; nowhere do we pretend and act as if we are independent from God so much as when we are trusting in our idols. Here the danger is compounded because the inherent blindness of idolatry inhibits us from perceiving the hazard to our souls. What we must come to see, within this dynamic, is that the experience of human tragedy is the violent stripping of our idolatrous pretences. In tragedy, our idols fail us catastrophically, and we are made radically, painfully humble in the process. And it is precisely in these moments of tragedy when God speaks to us most clearly about these false edifices; yet it remains these moments when we doubt His voice most.

Hence, it is not so much that God is silent as it is that we just don't like it when He says "No" to us. In reaction to His

"No" we accuse Him of silence. We have made idols of our needs—we are worshiping what God can give us more than we are worshiping God Himself. We are choosing the gifts of God rather than the Giver of the gifts. And God refuses outright to give us things that will keep us from experiencing Him. He will not give us our idols because to give us those would be to destroy us. No matter how much it hurts us in the moment, God knows that caving in to our idolatrous requests would only kill us in the end. And God loves us too much to do that.

Having thus exposed the idolatry of our hearts, we are faced with two possibilities. We can wait for tragedy to strike and remove the idol for us. We can wait for the humbling that comes with the violent stripping of pretence. And, let me assure you, without exception tragedy will strike, for all human securities are guaranteed to fail. Alternatively, we can choose now to break our own idols and place our trust in God. We do not need to wait for tragedy to right the foundations of our lives any more than we need to wait for specific needs to need God. As becoming needy is a process independent from individual needs, so righting the foundations of our souls is a process independent from the experience of tragedy. We can right our foundations at this moment, without having to experience their violent smashing first.

How will we do this? We right the foundations by establishing our lives on Christ alone. After all, humans are made for security, and He is the only true security in our universe. All other things are guaranteed to fade: health, wealth, fame, civil states, children, the future. Indeed, all these things will be idols if Christ is not first in our hearts. Therefore in a real, practiced, and regular way we must anchor, root, and entrench our very souls in Jesus Christ and him alone.

We begin this anchoring process by learning who God is in the reading of His scriptures. We continue it when we create space for Him to speak and deal with us in silence. But the height (or depth, perhaps) of our anchoring is based upon the willing and complete surrender of our lives to Him. We must take stock of, and hand over, each and every aspect of our lives to Christ. We must die to ourselves; and hence Jesus offers this command, "If anyone would follow me and be my disciple, let him die to himself, and let him take up his cross every day, and let him follow me" (Luke 9:23, author's translation). We must, according to Jesus, crucify the self every day. And in this bizarre form of daily Christian suicide we sacrifice on God's altar every security that is not God alone. We give over all worry and fear, all ambition and desire, all dreams and failures. We must, like Abraham, offer our dearest possessions—our Isaacs—to God on the altar of sacrifice (Genesis 22). We've got to break our own idols. We must affirm, with C.S. Lewis, that we want "Not my idea of God, but God."[*] In principle this is no different than the process, discussed earlier, where we attend to our human anxieties so that we can offer them to God in prayer—where we offer God control of our lives. Except that now we are attending to our idols so that we can offer *them* to God in prayer. The principle is the same; it is only the scale that is different.

God is not silent, but we are deaf. And we are deaf, ultimately, because we are idolatrous. We are idolatrous when

---

[*] C.S. Lewis, *A Grief Observed* (San Francisco: Harper Collins, 2001), 67.

we pray to a god that isn't God, but this idolatry is corrected—
our ears are opened—through the reading of scripture. We are
idolatrous when we fill our lives with noise so that we cannot
hear God's voice; we become deaf and dumb like the idols with
which we have filled our time. We correct this idolatry—we
open our ears and eyes—through dedicated periods of silence.
Lastly, we are idolatrous because our requests themselves are
idolatrous. We pray for things which are directly opposed to
God's plan for our lives; we have made idols of our needs. We
correct this idolatry—we open our ears—through offering
ourselves in complete submission to Christ; we die to ourselves.
These three disciplines—Scripture, Silence, and Submission—
are essentials to righting the foundations of our lives, establishing us upon the true cornerstone of God's will, and enabling
us to hear His voice in all its fullness.

Questions for Group Discussion

What are some distractions that keep you from hearing God's voice?

Has disobedience to God ever played a role in your experience of His silence? Tell the story.

Have you ever heard God speak to you, clearly, through the reading of the scriptures? Tell the story.

What are some practical ways you can engage in Scripture, Silence, and Submission?

V

ANSWERS TO PRAYER, PART 2
The Gift and the Giver

There is an old story about a man whose home was in the path of a rising flood. After the local authorities gave the order for evacuation, the police came, knocked on his door, and instructed him to leave. The man refused to go. Instead, he informed the officers of his firm faith, saying, "God will save me." The waters rose around his house. After a while, some men with a boat came by and urged him to leave with them. Once again the man replied, "No, God will rescue me." The men floated off and the waters continued to rise. In time, the man was forced to climb to the roof of his house to escape the flood. A helicopter arrived with a rescue squad, lowered ropes and ordered the man to come with them. Still he refused, adamantly restating his conviction that "God will rescue me." The flood continued to rise, and the man was swept away along with his house and died. In heaven, he complained bitterly to God: "God, I trusted you to rescue me and you didn't!" But

God said to the man, "I sent you a policeman, a boat, and a helicopter—what more did you expect?"

Some of you (possibly many) are rolling your eyes at that old fable. It is, of course, a ludicrous story, but it nevertheless opens the door to an important question: How do we know God's voice when He speaks to us? The man in the joke is looking for something overt, like a heavenly sign or an audible voice; he's looking for direct, divine intervention. Is that what we're supposed to look for when we pray? Or are we supposed to attend to more subtle ways of speaking? If God's voice is indirect (for example, through policemen, boats and helicopters), then how do we know when it is God speaking and not our imaginations? And when it comes right down to it, when we ask God for specific things (that is, if I make a specific request), should I look for a specific or an indirect answer to my prayer?

The previous chapter sought to prepare our ears to hear God's voice; this chapter will focus both on knowing God's voice when He speaks and the kinds of answers that He gives. We have cleared our ears, as it were, and now it is time to tune in to God's voice. In the first part of this chapter we will focus on discernment—with knowing God's voice. We will begin here because God speaks to us both directly and indirectly; as a consequence, we must have a way both to navigate between the subtle and the overt and to distinguish between God's authentic voice and our imaginations. In the second part of this chapter we will examine the three types of answers God gives us (Yes, Silence, and No). God does indeed answer our prayers—not only that, He answers them specifically; for our part we must prepare our hearts to receive the kinds of answers that God provides. In the end, when we recognize the sound of God's voice and are attentive to the answers that He gives, we are prepared to receive His answers to our prayers.

KNOWING GOD'S VOICE

It is a basic presupposition of this book that God is speaking to us all the time. It is also assumed that you are a person who desires to hear God's voice in response to your prayers; you are, in other words, a person who craves answers. Here I must stress again the three disciplines of the previous chapter—Scripture, Silence, and Submission. These are invaluable prerequisites to knowing God's voice when He speaks (and one of the main reasons why this chapter is "part two" of answers to prayer). Of these, Scripture is the most important factor—it is the primary way God communicates His will to us. But the Scriptures, while primary, are by no means the only way God speaks. They are authoritative, and all other forms of speech are measured by them, but they are not God's only method of communication. Far from it—the God Who created the universe speaks to us in an unlimited variety of ways; it is precisely this variety that makes the question of discernment imperative. Therefore we must ask: How do we discern God's voice in these other places? What is its particular sound when He speaks to us? In the following section I want to discuss four such "alternative" ways that God speaks to us: the gift of peace, impressions upon our hearts, overt signs, and the Church.

In my experience, the most common way that God communicates with His people is through the gift of peace. God's peace is what we experience when we are living in God's will, in accordance with His desires. It comes upon us most powerfully when we have given our anxieties over to God—that is, when we have submitted our wills to His. But more than simple relief, God's peace is a supernatural sense of His power working through and controlling our lives. It is the attitude of our hearts when we are right with God and secure in His will. It is an inexplicable peace, because it is often completely independent from the circumstances in which we find ourselves. Our lives may be falling apart or in good order, but the peace of God will transcend our understanding at all points. From within God's peace we are equipped to make the most difficult decisions; it gives us the freedom to live our lives, fearlessly, as God wills us.

God gives and withholds His peace as a way to communicate His will to us. Therefore, one of the chief ways to discern God's will for our lives is to chase His peace. There are a number of ways to do this, but the simplest is to pay attention to our obedience. When we are out of God's will—that is, when we are disobedient—we experience un-peace. Then, when we shift into God's will, thus becoming obedient, we experience God's peace. One of the women in my church, in speaking about God's dealings with her, used language that I think is enormously helpful here. She spoke about having "burdens" from God—things He was asking from her, and of her. They would lay on her heart like a weight, pressing her with a sense of un-peace. Whatever the burden was, it was a place where God was asking for obedience on her part. When she obeyed God in these matters, the burden would lift and she would come into the peace described above. This process of burdens and peace illustrates an essential dynamic—almost like breathing in and out—of the voice of God operating in our everyday lives.

The next way that God speaks to us is through impressions that He places on our hearts and minds. The majority of times, I believe, when people say that God "spoke" to them fall under the umbrella of such impressions. These impressions can come to us through any means at all. God can speak to you through a conversation with a friend, something you heard on the radio or read in a book, through your devotions, at church or at work or in the car. The so-called "Holy Spirit Highlighter" (where a passage of scripture seems supernaturally illuminated and appropriate) is one of these impressions as well. God, remember, is not limited in how He speaks to us; neither, I should add, are we limited to listening for Him with our physical ears alone—no, we listen spiritually with our entire bodies. Because of this, we can attend to God's voice aurally, visually, experientially, or even in our memories. What you will find with these impressions from the Lord is that a word, a picture, or an idea is planted in the mind, or brought to you by someone else, and lingers there more than other thoughts you have. Similar to the "burdens" we just described, these words will have a sense of *weight*; they are special thoughts that mysteriously transcend all our common thoughts. The key will be to discern, once you've heard it, whether or not it is a word from God.

How do we effectively navigate these impressions? How, practically speaking, do we know when God is really speaking, and it is not merely the voice of others, or of our world, or one of our own making? I find the following six characteristics to be always true when it comes to God's authentic voice.

First, when God speaks, obedience is mandatory. He regularly, when He speaks to us, gives us something to do. Even when He doesn't give us a specific task—for instance, when He gives us words of comfort—those words must be *accepted*, and that acceptance is a form of obedience. Thus, when God speaks, He presents us with the option to either follow Him or ignore Him. It is possible that, if you haven't heard God speaking to you in a long time, it is because at some point you ignored a command and He's still waiting for you to obey it.

Second, the voice of God comes to us with extreme clarity. Many of our regular human thoughts and ideas are muddled and unclear, but thoughts that are God's voice for us have a special clarity about them. They even feel different from our regular thoughts. Teresa of Avila, in writing about discerning the voice of God, speaks of this clarity when she observes that thoughts from God come fully formed into the mind. By contrast, when I am inventing an idea, I have the sense that I am stringing the words together one by one.* A full thought, pressed upon us strongly from within, is one of the ways we can know it is God speaking and not our imaginations.

Third, the voice of God is memorable. I may forget the other thoughts of my day, but the words that God speaks to me stick with me clearly. Even years after the fact, when I have utterly forgotten conversations with others, I still remember clearly impressions that God laid on my heart.

---

* Teresa of Avila, *Interior Castle*, trans. by E. Allison Peers (New York: Image Books, 2004), 139. In fact, much of what I say here regarding discernment of the voice of God is explored in Teresa's Sixth Mansions.

Fourth (and once again), God's voice in your life will never contradict His voice in scripture. God is always consistent in His dealings with us. This principle doesn't mean that God only speaks through scripture, but rather that scripture and God's special voice are always in perfect concert with one another.

Fifth, arguing with the voice of God—balking at obedience—only makes the need to obey stronger and the message itself clearer. The more you fight, the more His will closes in on you. The more you argue with God's voice, attempting to blame it on a distraction, or a bad lunch, or feeling sick—in short, the more you try to get out of obedience—the more God's voice burns clearer in your heart.

Sixth, and finally, when we obey the voice of God we experience immediate peace. The pressure to obey is a powerful anxiety in our souls—an anxiety that is matched only by the relief we feel when we have obeyed God's command.

On one occasion I sat in a hotel lobby reading a book of spiritual direction while my wife was upstairs, putting our son to sleep. While I was sitting there, a man entered the lobby and sat in a chair near mine. I was attempting to mind my own spiritual business, but God placed the impression on my heart that I needed to go and pray for the man. I tried to get out of it. I was tired, I reasoned, and I was not thinking clearly. I prayed (ironically!) that the man would get up and walk away before I would have a chance to pray. But the more I resisted, and the longer I sat in my chair, the stronger the need to obey became. My pulse raced, my heart pounded, and I argued as strongly as I could with God. Finally, I agreed to go. I got up, walked over, and (stumblingly, I might add) told him that I felt like I should pray for him, and then did so. In truth, the conversation was awkward and stilted, and after I had sat down we exchanged furtive looks until he left the lobby shortly thereafter. Despite this, when I was done I had a strong sense of God's peace. I had done what was asked of me, even though I didn't (and still don't) understand it. God spoke; I obeyed.

There is another way that God speaks to us, and this is directly through overt signs—whether an audible voice, miraculous signs, visions, dreams, or other means. Here we come to a curiosity: while God speaks to us constantly through peace and the scriptures, and while He speaks a little more rarely (but still quite often) through impressions that He lays upon our hearts, these overt signs are even rarer. What we must come to understand is that the only real difference between these more "special" revelations and the quieter, constant voice of God is volume. It is the same God Who speaks, with the same unchanging character informing His voice. As a result, there is no functional difference between hearing God one way and hearing Him another, whether God speaks to you quietly through your devotions, or loudly through an audible voice. One way is not better than another, and in each case the mandate to obey Him is the same. The only real difference is that the louder the voice God employs in your life, the greater the obedience is asked of you. Hence, if you are a person who craves to hear the voice of God in one of these special ways— dreams, visions, signs, or an audible voice—then you must also be prepared to obey Him radically.

How will we know legitimate signs from imagined signs? Remember, it is the same God speaking, and therefore the same criteria of evaluation can be applied to the overt signs as are applied to the more indirect impressions. Every instance, then, when we hear God's voice follows the same guidelines outlined above: the need for obedience, clarity, memorability, scriptural concord, pressure for obedience, and peace.

After university my wife and I were unsure about the next step for our lives. We knew that I wanted to continue my studies, and we had determined together that seminary was the right choice, but which one? We considered several different schools, but none stood out. Then one day we were eating a meal with one of our pastors who mentioned, in passing, that Regent College was a place to consider. His words promptly went in one ear and out the other, and I didn't give it a second thought. Then, some weeks later, I sat in a chair in my apartment finishing a book that I really enjoyed. I read the last page, placed the book on the coffee table next to me, and sat back satisfied, thinking to myself, "That was a really great book!" As sometimes happens, the paperback cover of the book had peeled back from the tension of holding it open, leaving the title page exposed, and as I looked over at the volume again I saw—no, 'saw' isn't the right word—some words *leapt* off the page at me: "Published at Regent College, Vancouver, British Columbia." Suddenly I knew, really knew, unmistakably knew, that Regent was the seminary I needed to seriously consider.

Did I hear an audible voice? No. Did I find my answer in scripture? No. But God planted a word for me to see, highlighted it by His power, caused it to transcend my usual thoughts, left me with a need to obey Him, made it clear and memorable, and through these means (and others as well) guided my family to the seminary He wished me to attend.

There is a final, indispensable way to discern and confirm the voice of God, one that stands above, through, and alongside all these other means: God confirms His word for us through the Church. A faith community uniquely allows us to test the voice of God in our lives. How does this work? Others will know more scripture than you and will have had other experiences with God than you. Others will be able to either confirm or question what God is saying to you. And in knowing both you and the God Whose voice you desire to hear, they can offer informed advice on what God is really saying *to you*. What is more, as vessels of the Holy Spirit, each fellow Christian has a connection with God, just like you. I like to compare a community of prayer to a grouping of radio antennae, each tuned in to the Holy Spirit. The more people you have praying together, the more people are listening for God's voice together, and the more likely it is that you actually will hear Him speak to you.

Here we come to one of the miracles of God's voice in the world: God will give *me* a word for *you*. This should not surprise us, because God loves agency. He rarely does alone what He can do through someone else. After all, our God is a *sending* God—He sent His son into the world as His agent to bring the world back to Himself. As His adopted children, we become His agents in the world as well; vessels for divine use. Part of the joy of petitionary prayer is that when we do it we are offered the privilege of being participants in God's work in the world. Hence, God uses us as His messengers to one another. The advantages of this process are considerable: in one sense, by speaking through me to you, God can independently confirm His message to you. In other words, the use of more people increases the clarity of the word, and it does this because of the way that the Holy Spirit works in our lives. When God gives me a word to speak to you, it is the Holy Spirit in you that either confirms or rejects the word. If it is truly God's voice, the Spirit will supernaturally *accept* the word. Our hearts leap within our chests. We have a sense of *knowing* that God has spoken to us. And to describe this experience we use phrases like, "That really spoke to me," or "That resonates in my heart." But in addition to clarity, God's use of agency to speak to His people also gives us confidence. On my own, I am left to wonder if God has really spoken to me, and I live with a measure of insecurity. But when another person thinks God has spoken to them on my behalf, and the Spirit confirms it in my heart, then my confidence increases radically. Thus, we powerfully confirm the voice of God in community. But in a still deeper sense, agency magnifies God's glory in our lives. When God shares His power in this way, not only is the person who received the word blessed, but also the person to whom the message was given, and both of them in turn give glory to God for His loving care. You are blessed and glorify God because He spoke through me, and I am blessed and glorify God for the same reason! As a result, when God speaks this way in our midst—when He shares His power with us—it magnifies His fame and glory and our hearts are moved to worship. And each of these things—clarity, confidence, and worship—point to why the Church is an indispensable asset in the hearing of God's voice.

There is a final thing to be aware of when attending to the voice of God: God always speaks to us in the softest voice we are able to hear. If we are deaf, He shouts, but if we are attentive, He whispers. And hence, the majority of God's speaking into our lives happens in ways that aren't overt signs—flashes of light, visions, dreams, audible voices, and so forth. All of these things do in fact happen, but they are uncommon, while the small things are manifold. I believe that the quieter our lives become—through our attention and pursuit of God—the more we will hear God speak on a regular basis. When we open our ears and attend to His voice, we will hear Him as the psalmist heard Him: in the whole voice of creation. And it is only as we learn to truly attend to the voice of God that His unending and manifold witness will be revealed to us.

THE FIRST ANSWER: YES

All that has been said thus far in our discussion of hearing God's voice—of clearing our ears and knowing what to listen for—has been preparation for us to apprehend the answers God gives us in prayer. The question to which we turn now is this: What kinds of answers can we expect to hear from God in response to our petitions? There are three answers we receive to our petitions: sometimes God says yes, sometimes He is silent, and sometimes He says no. Each of these answers prompts a unique response from us.

The first answer to prayer that God gives us is yes. We offer a petition to God, and He gives us what we ask for. These answered prayers range from the overtly miraculous (God healing the sick, providing money where there was none, strangers with words from the Lord for us, etc.) to the mundane (getting us to work on time, helping us find our keys, and so forth). And seen this way, it becomes clear that God says yes to our prayers on a regular basis. We pray in our needs all the time, and God regularly answers our prayers with yeses.

But the "yes" answer to prayer is the least spiritually significant answer that God can give us. That is because when God says yes, there is a real danger that we will take His yes for granted. In fact, we already do. We pray all the time—God says yes all the time—but very often we pray and then forget our prayers. We ask God to do things for us, and don't attend to Him to see how He's going to answer us. Even when He does say yes, how often do we really respond to God's frequent yeses with gratitude? Sure, people are grateful when God answers so-called "big" prayers, but to what degree does a consistent gratitude run throughout our daily spiritual lives for all the things God does for us on a regular basis? This fact points to the deeper danger in the yeses of God, because in giving us what we ask for there is always a risk that we will clutch the gift and neglect the Giver. We will ungratefully take God for granted, assuming His help, demanding it when necessary, unappreciative when He does things for us. This, in fact, is how we most often go about our lives.

Two examples from the scriptures will elucidate this further. In Luke chapter 17 we read about ten lepers who came to Jesus and asked for healing. Jesus sent them to the priests, and on the way their leprosy was cured. Only one of the ten, however, returned to Jesus to thank him. And I suspect that this story points to a few things that are perennially true about the nature of gratitude. First, gratitude is uncommon— probably only one in ten people is truly a grateful person. And second, most people are ungrateful because they are unmindful.

They just aren't thinking about what God has done for them. The same is true for us.

A second scriptural example is found in the rebuke of Psalm 50:22-23 (NIV), where the psalmist says: "Consider this, you who forget God, or I will tear you to pieces, with none to rescue; He who sacrifices thank offerings honors me, and he prepares the way, so that I may show him the salvation of God." Here then is outlined the danger of ingratitude—in forgetting God, we become people who miss out on salvation. By contrast, the sacrifice of thank offerings—thanksgiving to God—is the very thing that prepares us to see the salvation of God. Thanksgiving is the forerunner to salvation. It opens our eyes to see His work.

Against this ingrained and dangerous trend, the yes of God in prayer should always move us toward gratefulness. Therefore we must practice a mindfulness that will prevent us from taking God for granted; we must practice thanksgiving. Such an attention to God's work will fundamentally change our perspective on the work of God in our lives, and this in part is because the effect of thanksgiving is always cumulative; the more you practice gratitude, the more grateful you will become. Try this as an exercise some evening before you go to sleep. Sit in prayer and think of ten things you have to be grateful for. You may struggle for the first few things—gratitude doesn't come naturally to us. But once you've begun to think of things for which you can be grateful, the doors will open in your heart and mind. Once you get going, I assure you that you'll have a difficult time stopping at only ten. And the spiritual reward of this discipline is that when we actively pursue gratitude our eyes and hearts are opened to experience the everyday work of God more fully. Having cultivated hearts that are thankful, we will move from taking God for granted to a powerful and all-encompassing gratitude toward God.

Another discipline that cultivates gratitude is the keeping of a prayer journal, and this can serve as an antidote to our lack of mindfulness. Write down prayer requests—no matter how small—and then write next to them their answers. Then, if there's ever a time when you struggle to remember why you ought to be grateful to God, you can open the journal and review what God has done for you. In this way we can continue to celebrate God's yeses, lending encouragement to our present prayers as well.

THE SECOND ANSWER: SILENCE

The second answer to prayer that we receive from God is silence. This silence is an actual answer, and must therefore be differentiated from the silence we experience because of our human deafness (idolatry). There are times when we make requests and God is silent in response to them. To my understanding He responds in this way for a variety of reasons.

Sometimes God is silent to punish us, and this silence is linked to the silence we discussed in the previous chapter. In Amos 8:11-13 (NIV), the prophet describes a "famine of the word of the LORD"—it is a condemnation of God's people for their disobedience. They ignored God's word, so God was going to ignore them. But this kind of silence, I believe, is one that is easily resolved through obedience. God is quiet because we have rejected Him; all that is required of us to hear Him speak again is that we get right with God by doing His will.

Obey God where He has commanded you and you will once again hear God's voice.

Sometimes God is silent because we have asked for something that is directly opposed to His will. We ask for our sins. We pray for protection when we're engaging in unrighteousness, like asking for success in committing a theft, or adultery, or cheating. Or, more innocently, we pray for Him to give us something we want that He doesn't want us to have— like asking for one job when clearly He is leading us toward another. There are several things at play when we experience God's silence in moments like this. On the one hand God is silent because we are being belligerent; on the other hand, it is not so much that God is silent as it is that He has clearly said "no" and we're refusing to accept it.

Sometimes, God has instructed us to "wait." We have made a request, and it isn't yet the right time for us to receive what we've asked for. In my experience when God says "wait" He says it clearly—and it is important to observe that "wait" is not silence, but is rather an answer to prayer. The silence is what we experience between God's "wait" and His later answer. If I ignore God's answer, and accuse Him of silence when in fact He has given me a clear answer, then my real problem is not God's silence but my own disobedience. When God says "wait" we must respond with patient expectation.

Sometimes God is silent to our prayers because our prayers are nonsensical. C.S. Lewis, mourning the loss of his wife in *A Grief Observed*, writes the following:

Can a mortal ask questions which God finds unanswerable? Quite easily, I should think. All nonsense questions are unanswerable. How many hours are there in a mile? Is yellow square or round? Probably half the questions we ask—half our great theological and metaphysical problems—are like that.*

Lewis here pinpoints a frequent problem of our prayers: we have made requests which God does not answer because He *cannot* answer them; not because He does not love us, or is not powerful enough, but rather because the request itself was beyond the logic of the universe, or in violation of the unchanging character of God.

Sometimes God is silent, not because our prayers are senseless, but because we framed them poorly; in other words, we pray prayers that aren't specific enough. We pray things like, "God, make me happy" or "God, I want a career." But when our prayers lack specificity, it becomes nearly impossible to see when God has answered them. Fuzzy prayers get fuzzy answers; specific prayers get specific answers (and help us to know what answers to look for as well). And because we've asked for vague things, God cannot give us clear answers; hence His silence. At times these nonspecific prayers reflect a fear of intimacy; people pray for general things because they are too scared to share the important details with God. The vague requests serve to keep God from interfering in one's personal life. When I am praying with someone and I get the sense that that person is offering such "distanced" or "safe" prayer requests, I usually press them to get more specific in their prayers. Otherwise we will pray, but the person will not experience an answer.

---

* C.S. Lewis, *A Grief Observed* (San Francisco: Harper Collins, 2001), 69.

Consider also that sometimes God answers our prayers in ways that we weren't expecting, and I think this is most commonly true in nonspecific prayers. A prayer request like, "God, make me a better person" may very likely be answered by God allowing you to go through a period of profound suffering. Suffering, after all, is how character is most often developed. The suffering God allows you to experience may prompt you to pray, in distress, "Why is this happening to me, God?" when the answer, all along, is that you requested it. One of my friends once prayed, "God, teach me humility." As a direct result of his prayer God brought him into a period of sustained and painful humiliation. In the midst of his distress he recalled what he had prayed, and realized the divine origin of his suffering! Consequently he decided to change his request. This time he prayed: "God, teach me vicariously through the mistakes of others." And it is true that often when we pray prayers such as "I want to be a better person," what we really mean is "God, I want to *feel* like a better person." We desire the rewards, without the work.

God's silence toward our prayers is a more spiritually significant response for us than His yes because His silence always presses us toward self-examination. We must examine, and reexamine, our requests. We must attend to the voice of God, speaking in our lives, and measure our requests against what we know of God's will. We must seek the counsel and prayers of community to help us get clarity in our requests. When we've gone through this process of self-examination we will narrow and modify our requests. As we know more about what it is we really want and how God is currently working in our lives, our perspective on what we need will change as well.

In this way, the silence of God serves to hone our requests so that we are asking for what we really need. I suspect that very often we do not hear answers to our prayers because we haven't yet been praying the right prayer.

Once, early in our marriage, my wife and I were in the middle of a major disagreement over an air mattress. She had loaned it to a coworker to use some weeks before, but now my mother wanted to borrow it for an upcoming visit. For my wife, the earlier commitment was more important; for me, the request of family was more important. In our argument, no amount of individual prayer on either of our parts had brought us a solution. Then, in a flash of spiritual clarity, my wife said that we ought to pray about the situation together. I don't remember what we prayed, but we both had a distinct sense of handing the issue over to God. Soon after, my mother called to say that she no longer needed the air mattress, and both of us had the profound sense that our prayer had been answered. God's earlier silence had pressed us into a different prayer—one that He was prepared to answer for us. In the same way, God's silence presses all of us into self-examination.

THE THIRD ANSWER: NO

The third and final answer that we receive from God in response to our petitions is "no." And this answer, far and above God's yes and God's silence, is the most spiritually significant answer we can receive from Him.

This may sound strange at first, but consider, for a moment, that three of the greatest moments of recorded prayer in the Bible are answered with God's no. Job lost everything of value in his life and turned to God for answers. In utter tragedy he turned to God and prayed, "Why?" But God gave no answers to Job's requests; instead, to Job's many petitions for an explanation, God said no. Jesus, in the Garden of Gethsemane on the night before he was crucified, prayed earnestly —so earnestly that it is likely the capillaries in his eyes burst and he wept tears of blood—that God would allow the cup of suffering to pass from him. "Father," he prayed, "If you are willing, take this cup from me; yet not my will, but yours be done" (Luke 22:42 NIV). Jesus asked for a pass on the crucifixion, and God said no. Similarly, recording a vision where he was raised spiritually into heaven, Paul speaks of how three times he petitioned God to relieve him from his mysterious thorn in the flesh (2 Cor 12:7-10). We do not know the nature of Paul's thorn, but we do know God's answer to Paul: He said no. Each of these prayers point to something of deep spiritual significance for us.

Why are these spiritually significant prayers? Because whenever God says no to our requests, He also clearly says yes to the offer of Himself. In exchange for the thing or circumstance we had requested, God offers Himself in its place. Job doesn't get an answer, Job gets a vision of God. Jesus doesn't get a pass on the crucifixion, he gets God's comfort through the crucifixion and his exaltation through resurrection. And Paul isn't healed, but receives the power of God to fill up the gaps in his weakness. With each prayer the petitioner received not what he asked for, but something greater in its place. And what we must come to understand, deeply, is that the first and greatest answer to any prayer we can offer is that God would give us Himself. The building blocks for this realization have already been laid—we have already seen how behind every human need, if we have but the wisdom to perceive it, is our greater need for God. We have seen how each ordinary need in our lives is an opportunity for us to experience and know God more. And nowhere is the offer of God Himself as the answer to our needs more apparent than when God says no to our requests.

In saying no, God refuses to give us gifts that would rob us of the true experience of God Himself. He refuses to allow us to settle for the gifts—as marvelous as they may be, but nevertheless mere castings off of God's glory—when we have all of God to experience and savor in our lives. It is ultimately when God says no that we must clearly and truly choose between the gift and the Giver of all gifts. "Job does not love you for you," Satan accuses God, "But because you have given him good things. Take away his gifts and he will deny you" (Job 1-2, paraphrased). That was Job's test, and it is our test as well in the face of God's no—will we accept the gift of God Himself in place of all the things God can give us?

And it is precisely here that the prayer lives of Job, Jesus, and Paul shine so brightly for us—given a choice between the gifts of God and God Himself, they each chose God instead. Job remained faithful even when God's silence and no seemed loud enough to break him. Jesus took the comfort of God Himself *through* suffering, rather than the escape from it. And Paul, in response to the no of God, rejoices and celebrates the power of God all the more; power which now shines through his weakness. They didn't get the answers they wanted; they got God Himself instead.

A further truth is embedded in these prayers: in each case the person's prayer was heard. God acknowledged the prayer as received, then said His no to it. Paul, Jesus, and Job; each were *heard* by God. And this reveals a fundamental truth about prayer: it is more important that we be heard than it is that we get what we want. Being heard in prayer affirms our relationship with God. When we are heard we are acknowledged; we are considered worthy of God's attention. And when we are heard, and heard especially by a loving and sovereign God, then we are equipped to trust in His goodness regardless of our circumstances or the particular outcome of our prayers. And from the safety and security of God's perfect love, a love that loves us enough to say no to our requests, we will be strengthened to receive from God whatever He has planned for our lives—be it suffering or joy. In the end, being heard—knowing that we are loved and experiencing that love in the self-giving of God to us—is what prayer is really all about.

Here God's offer of Himself in the place of our requests should lead us to worship. This is the pattern in which Paul leads us in 2 Corinthians 12, because he worshipfully celebrates the "no" which permits him to experience more of God. This should be our response as well, because the gift of God Himself is the ultimate object of our faith. He is the fuel of our Christian walk; He is what motivates and gives force to our prayers. And when God gives us Himself as the answer to our prayers, we receive a foretaste of what is promised to us in the future. We get glimpses of our union with Christ; we enjoy appetizers of our unity and communion with God; we experience but a portion of the ultimate and supernatural right-relatedness which is promised to every believer in Christ; we take part in Heaven's *shalom*. When God gives us Himself, we get a taste of heaven now, and tastes of heaven always make humans worship. The self-gift of God is the greatest answer God can possibly give to any request, and it is the one prayer request to which God always answers yes. When we ask for more of God, God always obliges us. And we, when we have accepted this yes of God, laying aside all gifts and expectations, all pride and pretence, all power and anxiety, all the answers we wish for and all the circumstances of our lives we cannot control, in the embrace of God Himself we will be able to do nothing else *but* worship. Our prayers and our worship will then be one.

Worship, in the Bible, is always linked with sacrifice, and saying yes to God's no is the deepest sacrifice we can make as humans. This sacrifice is severe because the true, full, sacrifice asked of us as followers of Jesus is a matter of offering all the good of our lives to God. In this life of complete self-sacrifice, Jesus is our pattern and model. George MacDonald observes, when commenting on the temptation narrative of Jesus, that it was impossible for Jesus to be tempted with evil—Jesus was too pure to be deceived in that way. Satan's tactic, rather, was to tempt Jesus with good—feeding the multitudes would be good, providing signs to help belief would be good, and inheriting the nations would also be good. Each thing that Satan offers Jesus is a good in itself, but is a temptation because the good is outside the will of God at that time. After all, Jesus does feed the multitudes, provide signs, and inherit the nations —he merely doesn't do it Satan's way. And what is tested, therefore, is the will of Jesus to do his Father's will in his Father's time, and not his own; to submit even his desires completely to God. Thus, the severe lesson that the temptation narrative teaches us is that our desires, no matter how good or noble on their own, are unmitigated, Satanic evils if they are outside of God's will. No good thing is truly good if we have seized it for ourselves independently of the command of God.* Therefore, when God says no to our desires He is asking us to sacrifice those desires to Him. And in response we must say yes to God's no. We must let go of those deep desires and dreams by offering them to God. Then, when we have done this, our self-offering will be complete. As long as we reject God's no, our desire—no matter how noble—will be an idol placed between us and God. We will be clutching our dream, and our dream will keep us from experiencing God.

C.S. Lewis's *The Magician's Nephew* contains what is perhaps the most spiritually tender moment in the entire *Chronicles of Narnia*. Digory is a young boy with a dying mother who embarks on an adventure through various different worlds. Along his journey, Digory awakens an evil witch and then drags her with him into the land of Narnia in its first hours of existence. Her presence threatens to undo the good that Aslan has created, and, in order to right his wrong, Aslan sends Digory on a journey to a sacred garden where there is a sacred tree, an apple from which will have the power to heal the land. But Digory is tempted on his journey, because the witch informs him that the apple which has the power to heal Narnia also has power to heal his mother, and he is inwardly tormented. He could escape, and heal his mother, but that would mean disobeying the Lion. He must make a choice between

---

* George MacDonald, *Unspoken Sermons, Series I, II, III* (Whitehorn: Johansen, 1997), 84-109.

desire and obedience. Digory chooses to obey Aslan, and brings the apple faithfully back to him. What strengthens Digory to make his choice is something he sees in the eyes of Aslan. Lewis writes:

> Up till then he had been looking at the Lion's great front feet and the huge claws on them; now, in his despair, he looked up at its face. What he saw surprised him as much as anything in his whole life. For the tawny face was bent down near his own and (wonder of wonders) great shining tears stood in the Lion's eyes. They were such big, bright tears compared with Digory's own that for a moment he felt as if the Lion must really be sorrier about his Mother than he was himself.[*]

God knows the pain of our self-sacrifice. He knows what it costs us to hand our deepest selves over to Him. He Himself, mysteriously, wondrously, has done it in Christ. What gives us strength to obey is the certain knowledge of God's perfect love, surrounding, encouraging, and indeed weeping on our behalf. And the choice in Digory's heart is a snapshot of the choice we face between our deepest desires and obedience to God. Which way do we go? When what is most valuable to us is on the line, do we choose God, or our desires?

The Pharisees and religious leaders stood at the foot of Jesus' cross and cried, "Save yourself!"[†] They continued, as they had throughout Jesus' ministry, to ask for him to perform a miracle to their satisfaction—they wanted God on their terms, rather than God on God's terms. They refused to accept with

---

[*] C.S. Lewis, *The Magician's Nephew* (New York: Macmillan, 1970), 142.
[†] See Matthew 27:39-44

gratitude the yes of God in Christ, and their reward was the silence of God. They demanded, in deafness and blindness, idolatrous requests of Christ on the cross, and received as an answer only silence. They rejected God Himself in favor of the idol of God they had created in their hearts. They refused to hear God's no, and lost out on the joy and fellowship that God offers to all who will truly hear Him.

We also stand before the cross and must make a choice, because the cross is the moment when God's no is most profoundly also God's yes, when His rejection of sin is also the offer of Himself. And we must decide if we will willingly crucify all our desires and plans, putting to death all the idols of how we think the world ought to be run in glorious exchange for the One who runs the universe. Will we judge this cross by the standard of the Pharisees—in ingratitude and idolatry? If so we will miss the Giver of all gifts.

In all this we must come to see that our need, our humility, our surrender, our fasting, our confession, our silence, our reading of scripture, and our submission—all the difficult work of prayer has but one true goal: God Himself. And the petition of all petitions, the request behind all requests, is the one to which God always answers yes: "God, give me Yourself." Do you have the courage to pray it?

Questions for Group Discussion

Have you ever heard God speak to you? Were the factors that confirm His voice, as described in this chapter, present in your experience? Tell the story.

Can you think of a time when God said yes to your prayers?

Can you think of a time when He was silent?

Can you think of a time when He said no?

VI
THE SCENIC VIEW
Submission and Providence

Drive in the mountains and you are likely to happen upon a sign marked "Scenic Viewpoint Ahead." If you have stopped to appreciate such a place you've been rewarded with an opportunity to stretch your legs, a tasteful sign informing you of the history or natural properties of the region, and, of course, a spreading, breathtaking vista. Mountains are framed by trees, the valley below yawns green and winding, and the whole perspective provides a vision of your journey that, by driving straight through, you would have missed. I always marvel at the cars that speed past without stopping.

In much the same way, this book has reached a kind of scenic height. Beginning our climb from the humble origins of human need we have ascended to the great, rarified heights of self-sacrificing worship. From this vantage point, then, we ought to pause and avail ourselves of the view which offers fresh insight into key features of our journey—features, of course, that have been ever-present yet obscured by proximity. We cannot see the mountains sometimes because the mountains themselves obscure our view; from atop them, however, we see our journey with a different clarity. Looking back, we can see two things about prayer.

The first feature to observe is that embedded in every prayer request is actually *three* requests. We have already noted that some need in our lives is the motive of every prayer. In concert with these need-promptings we offer, first, our *request* as a response to our need: "Father, I have a need. Please fill it." Following on the heels of our request, however, we must also offer God *the need itself.* If we offer the request, but clutch to the need, we will be holding to our perception—that is, how we *feel* God should answer us—more than God's reality. In such a scenario our needs will matter more to us than the God from Whom we are seeking answers, and we will have made an idol of our need. Here we pray, "Father, take my need"—or, in the language of Jesus' Prayer, "Not my will but Yours be done." Finally, there is a third request, deeper yet than the initial two, that in addition to the particular request and then the need itself we would offer to God *our very selves* as well: "Father, take me."

Let me offer you a few examples. I love my son and pray for his life and faith. I feel, deeply, the inadequacy of my ability to care for him, and in need I turn to God with my request: "God, care for my son." But in addition to offering the request I must also offer my need, and so I offer God my son as well: "God, he is Yours to do with as You please." Then, in addition to both of these, I must offer myself: "God, I am yours to do with as You please." My need to be a good father leads me in prayer to offer myself to God.

A girl who loves Jesus is in love with a boy who does not. Her need and request is simple: "God, bring my boyfriend to know You." But in the same way that she offers the request, she must also offer God the boy: "God take and do with him as You please." And, right behind this request and the need, she must offer herself: "God, do with me as You please." Only in that final submission will she discover God's loving will for her life.

Dissatisfied with my job I pray to God for a new job—my need motivates my request: "God, provide me with a new job." But along with my request, I offer the need as well: "God, I give you my present job—change my heart about it; make me peaceful; grant me the wisdom I require to serve You here." And throughout this process I must offer myself to God as well: "God, wherever You send me, I am yours."

Concerned because a family member has been diagnosed with cancer we pray: "God, heal my father." Then we pray, offering the need itself to God: "God, do with my father as You please." Finally, we offer ourselves: "Father in heaven, my life and his life are both in Your hands; do with us as You please."

In each case it is through this treble path of prayer—a need prompting a request, which in turn prompts the offer of the need, which in the end prompts the offer of one's self—that we learn to practice submission to God in all things. From the raw, ordinary material of our lives, from our common human needs, from the daily cravings in our bellies to the greater longings of our dreams to the desperate needs of tragedy, each experience is an opportunity for prayer which can lead to submission. Each prayer is an opportunity to experience God. The path, then, of petitionary prayer outlined in this book is a lifestyle of submission, successively offering our whole being to God at the heartbeat prompt of our ordinary needs.

The second feature of prayer we observe from the heights is the providence of God. This is a sensible place to speak about providence, because providence, as belief in God's supernatural superintendence of our lives, it is a doctrine that *demands* perspective. It looks down on the entire landscape of human existence; it is clearly a doctrine of the heights. Because of its otherworldly height the only moments when we can perceive it are moments when we ourselves draw near to those heights. Therefore providence is the doctrine of the mountains through which we've journeyed, mountains which are the very fabric of our travels, but only truly perceivable at rare viewpoints. In the same way providence has been continually present throughout in our discussion of prayer. Though we see it as through a glass darkly, it is the ground on which we've walked, if only because the very idea of prayer assumes the presence of a God who answers prayer. When God answers, he has *provided*.

Providence is the doctrine that declares God's provision for our lives. He answers prayers. He has a plan. It is a doctrine that declares that the events and circumstances through which we journey are imbued with an ultimate and definite *sense*, a meaningfulness that will become clear in God's good time. Providence is the doctrine of divine sight in the midst of human obscurity. Because of this it asserts two things at the same time: first, that I do *not* know what is going on, but second, that God *does* know. In declaring this divine knowledge to ourselves the doctrine of providence declares that the God to Whom we pray is worthy of our trust. What is more, to trust in the provision of God in the face of our limited knowledge is the heart of faith; how you live within the mystery of God's providence *is* faith.

The life of faith, framed by these heights, can be seen as an act of submission to God's providence. At the same time, it is our belief in providence that makes our submission to God possible. From within providence, when we pray we are trusting in, relying on, placing the foundations of our souls upon the belief that God superintends all the details of our lives. We believe that He Who is the Alpha and Omega, the First and Last, Who spoke the world into being at creation and speaks it into new creation at the end, is speaking into our lives right now. We also believe that in Christ we, the Church, sit on the Throne with God in heaven, reigning with Him, and that He controls our fates. Thus, when we offer a prayer request we are praying in the arms of providence—trusting God for His answer, and proving our belief in providence through the opening of our mouths. God provides, therefore I pray; and I pray so that I might trust in God's provision.

Genuine belief in providence means that we accept His providence whatever the answer we receive in prayer. God's 'no', His silence, and His 'yes' are all part of His plan. From within our belief in providence, then, and in conjunction with the tri-part submission of self embedded within each prayer, we successively allow God more and more influence in our lives. When we submit in this way, when we have learned through practice to hand control of our lives back over to God—in short, when we have ceased from striving *against* God's plan for the universe and choose instead to become *part* of it—we are rewarded with perspective. Submission to God's providence leads to perspective, and perspective, if we pause at our scenic viewpoint and look out over the journey before and behind us, leads us to a deeper apprehension of God's providence. Through this journey of submission we become, by means of our petitionary prayers, participants in God's providential plan.

But in addition to making provision for and permeating our submission to God, the doctrine of providence is also a doctrine that gives us hope. The Christian basis of hope is one that has been sadly subverted by culture, because despite what we have been taught hope is neither wishful thinking nor is it earnest dreaming. Hope, rather, is certain knowledge of the future that gives us confidence in the present. In this, the resurrection of Christ is the central dogma of hope in the Christian life. We know, assuredly know, that our future is secure in Christ's resurrection, and therefore have *hope*, a confident regard in the present because of what we know about the future. Providence, rightly regarded, performs the same function in our lives.

To say, then, that "God has a plan" is not a simple platitude, nor is it a band-aid for suffering souls. Rather, it is a profound assertion that, given enough time and perspective—given, in fact, a scenic viewpoint—I believe I will see my circumstances with heavenly eyes, from the heights, and be enabled to submit to God's greater plan *through* my present circumstances. In short, that through ordinary prayer I might experience God through my everyday needs. The trouble, of course, is remembering and clinging to providence in the midst of our changing circumstances. And one of the chief difficulties of providence is that, because it is a doctrine of the heights, it is also the doctrine we are most likely to forget in the valleys. Our trials regularly obscure our vision of God, no matter how clear it may be. We are forgetful. And in the midst of our suffering we lose perspective; our vision narrows, and all we can see in those moments *is* our suffering. But from within these valleys having faith is a matter of clinging to what we know in the midst of our trials; it is remembering the landscape of providence from within the valleys of doubt. And from within those valleys the doctrine of providence gives us both hope and comfort, because we know that inasmuch as we desperately cling to the providence of God in the midst of our suffering, so also God clings to us. We are not alone.

Providence provides comfort to our present suffering because it invokes the power of eternal perspective; by the providence of God our present sufferings are framed or encircled. A dear friend of mine, Jerry Root, observes that each human has a series of deep, scarring wounds on our souls; places where we have been hurt by others. We each, he asserts, have somewhere between four and eight such places in our lives. Reflecting upon these deep wounds in his own life, he then observes that, given time, he can see that God has brought healing to some of them. Amazingly, though, he is aware not only of healing, but also redemption. In other words, into these places of woundedness God has brought mysterious good into being. If God is able, he reasons, to draw redemption out of some of these deep wounds in my life, then is it not reasonable to presume that given enough time—given, say, eternity—I can have a confident hope that all things, however grievous in this time and place, can be mended by the grace of God? This is a process of perspective; it acknowledges that I understand myself and my present circumstances only partially, but in the midst of those circumstances I choose to frame my pain within the word of God's love and goodness. In providence I cling to the hope of grace in the midst of suffering. I draw a giant circle around my problems—no matter how large or small—and having framed them with God's providence I can live with real hope.

Providence, then, doesn't eliminate suffering, but it does give it meaning. And the making of meaning is one of the primary drives of humanity. Viktor Frankl, Holocaust survivor and psychologist, pioneered a therapeutic method called *logotherapy*. It is a method which holds at its centre this deep human need to make meaning of our situations, and also proposes that meaning-making renders our suffering manageable. He writes, "In some way, suffering ceases to be suffering at the moment it finds a meaning, such as the meaning of a sacrifice."[*] Framed by perspective, suffering gains significance.

Frankl, however, is not alone in his observation, and his words echo in the language of the saints as well. Baron Friedrich von Hügel, a great Christian thinker and spiritual director, instructs us to live our lives with an attitude "full of prayer, full of self-humiliation, full of gentle attempts gently to will whatever suffering God may *kindly* send us."[†] And what he means is that in the application of our wills to God's will, in the submission of our attitudes to His revelation, there is a choice

---

[*] Viktor E. Frankl, *Man's Search for Meaning* (New York: Pocket Books, 1984), 135.

[†] Baron Friedrich von Hügel, *Letters from Baron Friedrich von Hügel to a Niece*, ed. Gwendolen Greene (Chicago: Henry Regnery Company, 1955), 136.

to actively *will* what God sends us, even be it suffering. "Of course," von Hügel observes further, "even very great sufferings would not, simply of themselves, purify us from even small evil habits. It is only suffering *meekly accepted, willed, transfigured by love of God, of Christ*—it is only such that will purify or cure anything."* Suffering on its own is meaningless—suffering to which the human will is directed into the hands of the divine will is glorified.

Others also speak to this profound truth. "Suffering, gracefully accepted," writes Takashi Nagai, "refines the human heart, and the experience of darkness sharpens the vision of the spirit."† Nagai was a Japanese convert to Christianity during the years prior to World War II. A resident of Nagasaki, he survived the atomic blast, but lost both his wife and city in the process. In the aftermath, though personally riddled with leukemia, he became in many ways a physician of the soul of Nagasaki. The words of faith that he writes, from his position of personal suffering, have a poignancy that is unmatched. The following words are written to his children:

> Some get themselves into a knot over the 'unfairness' of God's Providence. Why are some people afflicted with low IQs, handicapped bodies, weak physiques, material poverty? I don't know, but I can assure you of this: if all of us accepts[*sic.*] ourselves as we are, it is absolutely certain that a day will come when we can see how God's plans have been accomplished, and precisely through our weakness... Our talents and handicaps may differ greatly, but we are all equal

---

* von Hügel, 224. Emphasis his.

† Paul Glynn, S.M., *A Song For Nagasaki* (San Francisco: Ignatius, 2009), 225.

in this: each of us is born to manifest God's glory, to know, love, and serve him here below and share in his eternal life after death... My little children, you are no geniuses, and you have been called to a tough future. True, but if you make the vital decision to live humbly and lovingly, you will live fruitful lives and be happy.*

The frame of perspective, of finding a meaning in the midst of suffering, has vast power to change our attitudes within those moments of suffering. For the Christian, we choose to find our meaning within the scope of God's providence. We cry out, with Job, his words of painful faithfulness: "Though he slay me, yet will I hope in Him," but we also cry Job's words of hope: "I know that my Redeemer lives" (Job 13:15, 19:25 NIV). In this way a meaningful life is a life lived within God's plan. For Nagai, for von Hügel, and for Job, when we suffer within the certain knowledge of the goodness of God—that is, in surrender to His providence—then our suffering is transformed into worship.

These faithful men—Nagai, von Hügel, Job, and many others—have gone before us. They were men who paused at the scenic views of God's providence and saw clearly something of the fabric of the universe. They paused there to scratch their names in the signpost and then shout out—their voices resounding, echoing into the valleys where providence is least seen but most needed—words we are desperate to hear. Their words, if we let them, will lodge in our souls and prick us to remember God's truth in the midst of all circumstances. The words may appear to us as bright lights, or we may hear them

---

* Glynn, 238.

as the faintest whispers, but we must remember that as we cling to them, God clings to us.

Lastly, as Christians, we must always allow providence to have the final word on suffering. This, after all, is the pattern that our Lord Jesus sets for us. From the cross Jesus cries out "My God, My God, why have you forsaken me?" His words are not a cry of abandonment; rather, in quoting the 22nd Psalm Christ draws our attention to the work of God being accomplished in Christ at that moment. This is not abandonment. This is not despair. This is God's triumph through suffering; through *this*—this appalling, desperate, apex of human wickedness—God is bringing about His ultimate plan of grace spread wide to all the nations of the earth. We cannot hear Psalm 22:1 apart from Psalm 22:22-31—that praise and thanksgiving shroud the death of Christ, that the declaration of God's faithfulness and goodness are nailed there with Jesus, that the promise of God's mission to the world is presented in the form of God broken upon, for the sake of, that world. "For he," the psalmist cries, speaking of God, "has not despised or disdained the suffering of the afflicted one; he has not hidden his face from him but has listened to his cry for help" (22:24). The psalmist continues:

"All the ends of the earth
will remember and turn to the LORD,
and all the families of the nations
will bow down before him,
for dominion belongs to the Lord,
and he rules over all the nations.

All the rich of the earth will feast and worship;
all who go down to the dust will kneel before him—
those who cannot keep themselves alive.

Posterity will serve him;
future generations will be told about the LORD.
They will proclaim his righteousness
to a people yet unborn—
for he has done it" (22:27-31 NIV).

That is the meaning of Psalm 22, the meaning that Jesus attaches to his agony, and the meaning of the cross as well. Christ, in his moment of greatest apparent despair, himself drew a scriptural circle around his suffering, framing the cross in the providential plan of God as revealed in the scriptures. Providence had the final word on Christ's suffering, on Christ's mission, and on Christ's life itself; may it be so with us as well.

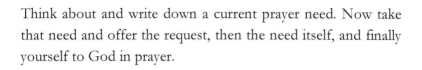

Questions for Group Discussion

Think about and write down a current prayer need. Now take that need and offer the request, then the need itself, and finally yourself to God in prayer.

What does this experience feel like?

Have you ever experienced a mountaintop view of God's providence in your life? If so, what did it look or feel like? How does that experience inform your times of doubt?

If you have never experienced a sense of God's providence, how do you respond to other people's stories of providence?

VII

PRAYING IN A GROUP
Tips and Protocols

So far we have talked about the essence of prayer—that it is about giving God control of our lives. We have described how to pray by pointing to the attitudes (humility, confidence, and boldness) that stand behind genuine prayer. And we've diagnosed our spiritual deafness and prepared ourselves to hear God's answers to our prayers. The only thing that remains for us to discuss is how to pray in a group. While I recognize, naturally, that each group of believers who gather together to pray will have unique characteristics and focuses, I want to take this chapter to describe how we, at my church, pray for one another. Perhaps there will be something here that you can use as you pray in your church. Perhaps not. Once again, let me state that there are no proper forms for prayer, only proper attitudes, and I pray that in your congregation you can find the freedom to invent your own ways of praying in a group. I offer no prescriptions here.

On Thursday nights a group gathers in my home to pray for each other and the work of God at our church. For those of us who regularly attend, our prayer night is something that has swelled in importance since we've begun it. It has deepened our faith. We have seen God move in our midst. We've watched how the direction of our congregation has been shaped by our regular prayers. At one point my church board, concerned about my busy schedule, attempted to suggest that I take Thursday nights off—prayer night—but of all nights I don't want to skip out on prayer. It's something I've come to need. When I can't make it, I'm truly missing something important.

Once people have arrived, we regularly do a few things as a group in preparation for offering our petitions. The first of these is to take a few minutes of silence so that we can still our hearts. Silence in communal prayer, I have observed, is indispensable, if only because the anxieties we each bring with us crowd loudly to the surface of our minds—traffic on the way, a bad day at work, an argument with a friend. The point of our silence is not to forget these things, but to make them subject to Christ. In the inner space of our souls we are each offering those worries to God so that we can better hear His voice in prayer. Silence is the first step of our preparation.

One custom I've picked up along the way is that of lighting a candle when the prayer group starts. I find that the candle serves two purposes. One is to remind us of the presence of Christ in our midst. After all, Jesus really *is* present, and it is important for us to remember this reality. A lit candle can help us physically to remember something that is always spiritually true. In the centre of our room, it also becomes a symbol of our community—we are gathered together around this little light, which in its own small way is a symbol of Christ, the true light of the world. The other purpose of the candle is that it can help someone who is struggling particularly with rogue thoughts and worries to focus. Instead of closing his/her eyes and wrestling with all the stuff going on inside, that believer can look at the candle, using its light to focus his or her attention.

Once we've lit our candle and sat in silence for a few moments, we sing together. Singing is one of the most important things that we do as a community. In the scriptures our songs are always bound together with our practices of thanksgiving—they are part of the new kinds of speech that are intended to characterize God's people (see Ephesians 5:19). As a part of our thanksgiving, songs open our eyes and ears to see and hear the beauty of God in our lives. But beyond even this, our songs of worship serve several purposes in the Christian life. One purpose is to make us aware of community. Songs stretch us outside of ourselves. We sing along with others, beside others. We live out our community in a real and powerful way when we sing together. Another purpose of singing is that, because we are responding to words that are true (the lyrics) with our bodies, it is as if we are physically assenting to things we believe in our heads. Singing is one of the key ways that we move truth from our heads to our hearts. To sing songs is to state, physically, that I agree with the truth of what I am singing. And a further purpose of singing is that it helps to focus our minds and hearts. When we are tuning our focus upon God, we are less focused on ourselves, and therefore will be better able to hear His voice in prayer.

A final thing we do before we pray is open the word together. Usually I will prepare a short (less than 5 minute) meditation on a passage of scripture. This can be as simple as a single verse, such as Habakkuk 2:20 (NIV)—"The LORD is in His holy temple; let all the earth be silent before Him." Or it can be something longer. We can focus on a characteristic of God, something Jesus has done, a teaching on prayer, or a story of answered prayer in the Bible. Something to remind our hearts and minds not only of the character of the God to Whom we are praying (something our songs should have done as well!), but also to remind us of the kinds of ways that He works in our world. Scripture offers us a heavenly perspective on what we are about to do, and we need a biblical vision for prayer if we're going to pray powerfully.

I should say that, as a rule, we regularly mix up the order of these three initial steps. Sometimes we begin with songs, other times we open with the scripture. The order is not important, but the content is. We need stillness, and worship, and scripture to right our hearts—or at least to point our hearts in the right direction—before we pray.

After these initial steps we have two more parts to our prayer night: we pray for each other—for our individual requests; and we also pray for our church—for the needs and vision of our fellowship as a whole.

I like to start with individual requests. When we first began our prayer group, we would go around the room and each person would share a request. As each person shared the person beside them would need to remember the other person's request. Then, once everyone had shared, we would pray in the circle, one person for another as we went around the room. This still works sometimes—I use it when we pray as a worship team before our church services—but on our prayer nights it began to feel clumsy and mechanical. It was also difficult for people to remember all the prayer requests.

And so, over the time we've been praying for one another, we've come to invent our own model of prayer. Instead of waiting for all the requests to be heard in the room, now we pray for one person at a time. In fact, we've adopted a kind of continuous prayer model. Here's how it works. Say Mary is sitting next to me, and Peter is sitting on the other side of Mary. Mary will share a request and immediately after she has shared it either Peter or I will pray for her. Once we've prayed for the first request, we ask if she has another. If she does, she shares that, and then the other person prays for her. If she has more requests, we go back and forth in this way, praying until we've offered all her requests to God together. When Mary is done, then Peter shares his requests, and Mary and whomever is seated on the other side of Peter will pray for him. We have a standing rule for the group that if, for any request, someone else (not seated next to Mary) feels led to pray for her, they know that they can say, "I'd like to pray for that too." And we all join in when that other person prays as well.

This new model has a number of advantages, one of which is that requests are kept fresh. The people praying are praying for the person in the moment. They aren't mulling over a request for some time, losing track of it as they hear other people's requests or forgetting it altogether. Another advantage is that it mirrors the inner process through which we offer our worries to God—one at a time. As those concerns are present to the person, we pray for them, and I think this makes the prayers more meaningful.

Whenever we pray for someone, the people on either side lay a hand on the person's shoulder. We always, of course, ask permission before doing this, but I think that the laying on of hands communicates some of the reality of prayer—rather than esoteric or imagined words, a real, flesh-and-blood person is offering a request to God on my behalf.

Two things need to be made clear about the sharing of requests. The first is in regard to confidentiality. It needs to be clear that what is shared in the prayer group stays in the prayer group. People need to have the security of knowing that what is shared will not be talked about, otherwise they won't feel the freedom to share. In fact, creating a safe community of love— where people will feel free to risk something of themselves for God—is the essence of a prayer group. For some requests, of course, members may want you to speak about and pray for them with others outside the prayer group, but those circumstances are naturally at the discretion of the person sharing the request. As a rule, one never talks about prayer requests outside of prayer group. When this happens it is, of course, gossip, and the Church must always be on guard against gossip in every circumstance. Gossip has the power to poison fellowship. I find that many people aren't sure when they are gossiping, so I offer them a handy litmus test for their conversations. Imagine that you are holding a conversation with Jane about Paul, who is not present. Now ask yourself this question: if Paul were listening to this conversation right now, would he be uncomfortable with what you're saying about him? If the answer is yes, you're gossiping and you need to stop.

The second thing to note about the sharing of requests has to do with asking follow-up questions. Sometimes it takes a while for an individual to shape his or her request. They are sharing about life but aren't sure what to pray for; they have a worry, but they haven't yet targeted the real source of the worry. It is okay to ask questions of the person sharing if the goal of your question is to pray more effectively for the person. It is permissible to ask questions for information. But what we must be alert to, however, and on our guard against, is becoming a group of counsel, rather than a group of prayer. If we don't watch against this, people will begin to give advice, when they ought to be offering prayers. Advice is cheap and easy to come by—everybody's got an opinion. But a prayer group is not about hearing human opinions, it's about hearing God's opinion. And the voice of God speaking in people's lives is something people are desperate to hear. Therefore the best thing we can do for any struggling believer is get them connected, in prayer, to the God who controls all things.

Let me try to make this concrete. Imagine that a person shares about a struggle they are having with a fellow student at school—they aren't quite sure what to pray for, but the worry is enough that they want to pray about it. The wrong kind of questions will attempt to resolve the issue through the giving of advice: "Have you tried this? What about this?" The right kind of questions will ask, "So, how are you feeling when you see this person?" or "What would you like to happen in this relationship?" Such clarity-seeking questions will serve to inform our prayers and help us to get to the Throne of God more effectively on the person's behalf.

If God speaks to you for someone else while you are in a prayer group—if He gives you something you think is a word from Him—test it out. First, ask God quietly to confirm whether this is a word He wants you to speak or not. You can pray, "God, bind my tongue if you want me to keep silent, but give me strength if you want me to speak." Second, if God confirms, or even if you're not totally sure, you can offer the word to the other person. It's a good idea to preface such a moment with a phrase like, "I'm not sure if this is God or not, but I think He's saying this to me." Perhaps God has given you a picture or an image that you can't shake, and He's asking you to share that as well. The key, I believe, is this: offer the word gently, and see what happens. If God has actually spoken to you, then the word will be accepted by the other person. He or she will receive it—the Holy Spirit in them will resonate with God's word spoken through you—and the speaking of the word will usually bring God's peace to the person for whom it was meant. On one occasion while we were praying I had a picture of a fish pop into my head. I knew, in that moment, that the picture was for a particular person. In a moment when we weren't praying, I brought up the picture and said, "I'm not sure if this is from God or not, but I think it might be for you." Her excited response was, "I had a dream last night that I was swimming in the ocean! I was actually going to mention it to you!" The word was given to me, but taken up and confirmed by her. (Incidentally, together we were able to determine that the ocean was God's Holy Spirit and the fish was her nature— it was an invitation from God for her to experience more of Him, which was pretty cool.)

In reading this description of our prayer group you may feel that such a focus on the individual isn't possible, if only for the simple reason that your prayer group may be much larger than mine. But there is a simple solution: break into small groups and pray for each other that way. Don't allow the enticement of "expertise" to limit your group's prayers for each other, as if you needed trained leaders to lead groups in prayer. All prayer, remember, is the business of amateurs.

Once everyone has had a chance to receive prayer for their individual requests, I usually offer a bathroom break, and we take a few minutes to share and fellowship again before we turn to prayers for our church.

Here again, when we first began our prayer group we had a way of doing things that has grown and matured over time. In the beginning, I wrote down a list of concerns and requests that pertained to our church—finances, vision, members, big dreams, concerns we had, our youth group, prayer group, and so forth. We would pass this list around the room and each person would pray for one item (or more) on the list. But once again, the process began to feel inorganic and laborious. We were "getting through the list" rather than talking to God. So, after some time, we threw the list out and changed our pattern. Now we begin our prayers for our fellowship in silence. And in silence each person prays for God to reveal a burden to us—we ask God to place on our hearts a need of our fellowship, something that we need as a community. Then, as the Spirit leads us, each person prays for the concerns that God has laid on his or her heart. As a rule we make a special point to pray for certain main issues (like financial needs or upcoming events), but the majority of our prayer is as the Spirit leads us, and I am often refreshingly surprised by what God leads people to pray. After all, each individual member sees our fellowship differently and experiences our needs differently. By canning the list and allowing us to pray this way—by unhooking control from our prayers—these prayers are now fresh and living. What was controlled and lifeless has become living and powerful.

Once the prayers have died down (I usually wait for an extended period of silence—between thirty seconds and a minute) I say a closing prayer and our prayer night is through. The end of formal prayer, of course, does not necessitate the end of fellowship.

That, in brief, is an evening of prayer at my church, and as a closing word I would like to assert once again the many great benefits of praying in groups. For many people their spirituality (and especially prayer) is a private, solitary affair. But we are in no way meant to do the Christian life alone, and in this a community of prayer helps us in a number of ways. It keeps us accountable in prayer, because attending a prayer group is a way to get yourself praying even when you don't feel like it. Group prayer reinforces our private prayers as well, because as our eyes and ears are opened we will become more accustomed to prayer as an everyday habit. Additionally, a prayer group helps us to remember our prayers. We, after all, are forgetful people, and we may offer requests one week and forget them by the next! But the community will remember, and ask on your behalf. A prayer community also helps us to give thanks— remembering your prayers, these fellow believers will celebrate with you when God answers you. They will mourn with you when you suffer; they will hear and advocate for you when you are in need. Need, remember, creates community—those who admit their needs must ask for help from others. We, as God's people, are made for community; in fact we are made to be needy for God. And when we recognize and admit our spiritual need for God and His Kingdom, when we admit it in community, when we begin to pray for one another, then that is precisely when together we are transformed into the Church of Jesus Christ.

Questions for Group Discussion

Can you tell the difference between "advice giving" and "going to the throne" in prayer for others?

Case Study 1: Jane comes to your prayer group and brings up a request about her relationship with her mother, which isn't going well. In this instance, Jane feels that she needs to remain single, but her mom is pressuring her to get married. What kinds of questions do you think you can ask to pray more effectively, and what kinds of comments fall under the category of "giving advice"?

Case Study 2: Peter has a coworker who is negligent in his work (he doesn't show up on time, uses company hours for personal business, is lazy, etc.). The problem is twofold—first, Peter ends up covering for his coworker's slack, and second, his bosses don't see the misbehavior of this employee. Once again, what kinds of questions do you think you can ask to pray more effectively, and what kinds of comments fall under the category of "giving advice"?

Do you know the corporate needs of your church so that you could pray for them?

EPILOGUE:
Beginning a Life of Prayer

I have endeavored to offer a short book on prayer, and yet I fear that I have failed; it is longer than I wanted it to be. The primary purpose of this book has been to encourage you to pray, to gift every believer with a vision for the ordinariness and everyday quality of the Christian prayer life. It is something, I am convinced at my core, that every believer can and should do. Standing against this purpose, the danger of length is that it creates, even implicitly, a culture of technicality and specialization. We have covered a range of topics. We've spoken at length about obedience, power, need, anxiety, and repetition. We've spoken about humility, confidence, and boldness. We've gazed at idolatry, scripture, silence, submission, providence, and community. And what I fear is that in the midst of all this knowledge you will think you need mastery of it before you can pray; that you require special technique, or skill, or spiritual aptitude, or confidence, or even right-relatedness to God as prerequisites. I fear that you will think you've got to have some things in order before you can begin your life of prayer.

The word with which I most desire to close this book is this: do not wait to pray. We *must not* wait to pray. Waiting to pray is another extension of our human desire to be in control, except that this time it is our desire to control the terms of our relationship with God. We want God, but we want to appear well-dressed, with our lives in order. We want Him to like us for the good things we've done. We want to show Him how good we are and be approved for these things. But our logic in this is as foolish as that of a sick man saying, "I think I'll wait until I'm well to go see the doctor." We dare not wait to come to God; we must come to Him as we are. You will never be "ready" to come to God. You will never be "in control" of your life in the way you envision in your mind. Your life will never be "right" enough for you to come to Him in prayer. And it most certainly won't get right by avoiding the very process by which God makes your life right. Therefore let nothing stand in the way of this invitation to experience God's power. In one of his poems George MacDonald wrote of prayer that he would not "put off calling till my floors be swept."* And we must say with him, "I won't wait, God, until I've got my life in order; instead I'll call you now." Lay aside your pride. Do not wait to begin the process of prayer. Do not wait to begin chasing your need for God. Start this instant.

And yet in the very same breath my pastoral heart presses me to urge caution. It is important to start small. We must begin our prayer lives, but we must also not bite off more than

---

* George MacDonald, *Diary of an Old Soul,* January 30.

we can chew. If you are going to train for a marathon, but have never run before, you must begin training. You've got to start running, but that doesn't mean you ought to run a full marathon on your first go. We must begin in small places and grow from there. But this is where many people unwittingly scuttle their prayer lives. Feeling guilty because they haven't prayed for some time, they re-start by attempting a marathon of prayer. The result is failure and discouragement, followed immediately by increased guilt because of their failure. When I counsel people in prayer I challenge them not to pray for hours at a time, but rather to find five minutes a day. You can pray for five minutes straight—whether it's the first five minutes of your morning or the last five minutes of your day; whether it's the five minutes in the car before you leave for work or the five minutes at the gym before you begin your workout. Choose a good time of day, when you are awake and alert, and not the last five minutes before you drift off to sleep. Give God a portion of your best self, not the leftovers. Begin small, set goals that you can achieve, and experience a little victory in your prayer life. You can always add more prayer. And all throughout this process we must remember that no one on earth feels adequate in prayer. No one on earth ever feels, when they are honest, that they pray enough. And the more earnest pray-ers you meet, the more honest about this fact they will be. You will never pray enough, you can only pray faithfully. And small, repeated prayers are the most faithful ones I can imagine.

Do not look down on the small. Do not think that the small is less valuable than the big. I believe that this is the very point of the mustard seed stories in the gospels: we ought not to look down on what appears small. The small, faithful act of planting a mustard seed—which appears so insignificant—reaps a reward far out of proportion to the seed itself. So also our lives of faith. And the key of spiritual growth is our commitment to these small, repeated acts of obedience. Will you be faithful in small prayers?

Prayer, and especially prayer in petitions, is the ordinary business of ordinary believers. It requires no prerequisites, special skills, or talents—only obedience. It is the common and everyday work of the Christian faith. It is small and oft repeated work, but its pursuit and repetition reap potent rewards. When we sow in petitions, the harvest we reap is the power of God in our lives, and more even than the power of God, the great harvest is God Himself. The reward of prayer is God. This, then, is the Christian spiritual life in a sentence: begin to pray, learn your need, and allow God Himself to be the satisfaction of your need. What are you waiting for? You have everything you need to get started right now.

Question for Group Discussion

During a conversation, a friend mentions his or her discomfort with the idea and practice of petitionary prayer. Now that you've read this book, how would you answer that person?

ABOUT THE AUTHOR

Jeremy Rios was raised in the American Midwest. He studied Greek and Latin at Wheaton College and has a Master's of Divinity from Regent College in Vancouver, British Columbia. From 2008-2013 he served as pastor of New Hope Alliance Church in Surrey, BC. Starting in 2013 he has served as Lead English Pastor at Burnaby Alliance Church. He is married, has three children, and loves cooking, reading, films, and great conversation.

For future book releases, contact information, and links to Jeremy's blogs, please visit www.jeremyrios.com.

Wonderfully and fearfully made
God is p You are perfect
in all of Your ways.

Printed in Great Britain
by Amazon

32156283R00099